A PREVAILING PASSION

A HISTORY OF WORCESTER FESTIVAL CHORAL SOCIETY

Mary Parsons

with an Epilogue by Donald Hunt

OSBORNE HERITAGE

Series Editor Michael Fardon

Osborne Heritage is the historical publishing division of Osborne Books Limited
Unit 1B Everoak Estate, Bromyard Road, Worcester WR2 5HN

Printed by the Bath Press, Avon.

British Library Cataloguing in Publication Data
A catalogue record for this book is available from the British Library

ISBN 1 872962 95 5

Cover picture Worcester Cathedral, circa 1880 (photograph Clive Haynes)

"The love of music . . .
one of the prevailing passions in Worcester"

Worcester Herald, 14 June 1865, reporting
a Worcester Festival Choral Society Concert

Dedication

by

Philip Goodrich, Bishop of Worcester

One of the many advantages in being Bishop of Worcester is the quantity of music there is, especially in the Cathedral. The choral traditions of Worcester, the Three Choirs Festival and much more, are integral to our life. In this the Worcester Festival Chorus is central, and as Bishop I am proud to be its President. Many are the stories to tell concerning its history and there is no better person to tell them than Mary Parsons, herself a former member of the Chorus.

+ Philip Worcester

September 1995

Acknowledgements

In collecting information and writing this history I have been much helped by the willing response, help and encouragement of many people: the staff of the British Library, Trinity College of Music, Worcester City Library, Worcester Record Office and the Elgar Birthplace; Vernon Butcher, Ruth Piggott and Ron Stratton (for access to records in the Cathedral library); John Phillips, Marjorie Potts and Wynne Tucker.

Donald Hunt has not only written the Epilogue, but has also read the draft of the book and made additions and emendations for which I am grateful. I am especially indebted to Wulstan Atkins for his help and hospitality, for reading this history and making suggestions and emendations, for his permission to reproduce published material referred to in the bibliography, and for his Foreword. I was delighted by the interest and enthusiasm shown by those whom I asked to contribute reminiscences: Jeannine Alton, Harry Bramma, Stephen Cleobury, Stephen Darlington, Richard Holding, Eric Kemp, Catherine King, John Langdon, Robert Milburn, Andrew Millington, Tom Pierce, Christopher Robinson, Henry Sandon and Paul Trepte.

To Anthony Boden and Harold Watkins Shaw go my thanks for their permission to quote from their books, and to the Oxford University Press for permission to quote from *Edward Elgar: A Creative Life* by Jerrold Northrop Moore and *Edward Elgar: Letters of a Lifetime,* also by Jerrold Northrop Moore. Thanks must also go to Edwin Roxburgh for illustrations from *The Rock* manuscript score. Acknowledgements for photographs in the text appear under each one. Special thanks must go to Roderick Attwood and Clive Haynes for research for these illustrations. Grateful thanks also go to Cyril Kemp for preparing the text, to Jill Bray and Anne Waugh for reading it, and to Michael Fardon of Osborne Books for editing and publishing it.

Finally, I owe very much to the friendship of past and present members of WFCS, to my memories of over forty years of singing, in Worcester and in the Three Choirs Festival, and to the resulting comradeship. This short history may serve as a small return for that rich experience.

Mary Parsons
January 1996

Contents

Foreword

by

E Wulstan Atkins MBE

Vice-President of Worcester Festival Choral Society

It is with great pleasure that I accept the invitation to write a Foreword for the History of the Worcester Festival Choral Society.

I have read the draft with keen interest. For the first time one can fully understand the ever-increasing part that the Society has played over the last one hundred and thirty five years in making music, not only in Worcester, but by its share in the Three Choirs Festival Chorus each year, over a much wider area.

As the book so admirably records, the Society followed earlier music groups in Worcester. It was expressly formed in 1861 to provide singers for the Three Choirs Festivals, which it has done, with the exception of a break of a few years after the 'Mock Festival' of 1875, during which time singers from other Worcester organizations, including the Worcester Philharmonic, supplemented the Festival Chorus. The Society was revived in 1887 and has faithfully provided singers ever since.

What memories this book evokes! When I was a Cambridge undergraduate I spent many happy Monday evenings attending rehearsals, sitting with Edgar Day at the piano, and over the years going to as many of the Society's concerts as I could. I have clear memories of a performance of *Elijah* in December 1925. Elgar, who loved *Elijah,* and came back to our house afterwards, told me how delighted he was with the performance, expecially the choral singing and the playing of the orchestra. Another vivid memory was *Gerontius* in March 1931. I can remember Elgar talking to Edgar Day in the North Choir aisle of Worcester Cathedral and saying that he would wander around during the rehearsal, which he did and indeed also during the performance. He hated sitting throughout concerts.

Mary Parsons has made a valuable addition to the books about music in the Midlands, and has filled in a previous serious gap in our knowledge.

A concert programme dating from 1860 (Worcester Record Office)

1

VICTORIAN MUSIC MAKERS

When Edward Elgar's father came to Worcester in 1841, he joined the Glee Club, which had met regularly in the Crown Hotel in the city since 1810. What songs they sang in the old coaching inn during the early decades of the century can only be guesswork, but there exist concert programmes for the 1850s which give many glimpses of Worcester's musical activities and enthusiasms in the middle of the century.

Whilst many of the players and singers in the northern bands and choirs were mill workers and manual labourers, in Worcester the performers in the city's concerts appear to have represented a different social background. In 1857, for instance, an 'amateur' concert included *Macbeth,* by Locke, with Hecate sung by Lieutenant-Colonel Bell; a number of solo songs sung in Italian, and 'a Grand Instrumental Selection from Verdi's new opera *La Traviata'.* The list of performers includes, as well as the lieutenant-colonel, the Honorable Mrs Talbot, and the Hon. Mrs Dudley Ward and Lord Ward, and there is a note that 'after the concert there will be dancing'.

An earlier concert in the same year is Mr J J D'Egville's Vocal and Instrumental Concert, with a solo violin played by one H H Cooper, solo violinist to the London Philharmonic Society, and the patrons' list printed in the programme is headed by the names of many well-known county families: Lord Ward, Earl Beauchamp, Lord Southwell, Sir John Pakington, Sir E A Lechmere, Sir O Wakeman, Mr R Berkeley and, representing a different kind of distinction, Sir Charles Hastings. In those class-conscious days, there followed the names of the rest of the patrons.

The number of music societies promoting concerts certainly testifies to one of Worcester's 'prevailing passions' – the love of music. A concert in 1854, for instance, was given by the 'Harmonic, Philharmonic and Madrigal Societies'. In 1857, there was a whole series of concerts in March and April, given in the Natural History Room in Foregate Street, by the Worcester Glee and Madrigal Union. The following year, also in the Natural History Room, there was a concert in honour of the marriage of HRH the Princess Royal. Among the instrumentalists is Mr H Elgar (Edward's uncle) and the interestingly-named Mr De Poix Durieux, whose wife's name is among the singers.

These singers and players, leading their apparently comfortable lives in a fairly small cathedral city, were not unaware of their less fortunate fellow-citizens, of their contemporaries in the dark industrial cities in the north, or of the sufferings in the Crimean War. In 1854 there took place 'a Grand Evening Concert for the benefit of the Coal Fund' and 'a Grand Amateur Concert for the benefit of the wives and children of the soldiers who have gone to the East'. Another Grand Evening Concert in 1857 was in aid of the funds of the Working Men's Institute, and in 1862 there was one in aid of the Lancashire Distress Fund.

What, it is now time to ask, did these music-makers sing and play? Handel was an undoubted favourite: his *Acis and Galatea* was performed several times, also his overture from *Saul* and a number of duets and solo songs. There were madrigals, songs by Beethoven, Haydn, Boyce, Bishop, a number of Italian songs, and, as a final number, 'Rule Britannia' with solo singer and chorus. Another choral work that appears on other occasions, as well as when Lieut-Colonel Bell sang Hecate, is Locke's *Macbeth,* the strange libretto of which owes little, if anything, to Shakespeare. Perhaps the most bizarre of all is a song from *The Maniac*, entitled 'The Tiger Crouches in the Wood'. The words are:

The Tiger crouches in the wood
And waits to shed the traveller's blood,
And so crouch we:
We spring upon him to supply
What men to our wants deny
And so springs he.

One imagines that these long programmes (for long they must have been) are a fair sample of music-making in the middle years of Victorian England. They included some works that today's taste finds delightful and some that are astonishingly crude. Whatever the content of the programmes, it seems certain that concert-going and performing were well-established activities in Worcester in the 1850s.

Ticket prices seem to have varied: for the series given by The Glee and Madrigal Union in 1857, front seats cost 1/-, back ones 6d, and children and schools half-price, but a little earlier that year tickets for the concert in aid of the Working Men's Institute were highly priced: 4/- for reserved seats, 2/- unreserved, with family tickets to admit six at £1 1s 0d.

The way was now well prepared for the formation of a Worcester Choral Society. The neighbouring town of Stratford-upon-Avon had established a choral society in 1836, the same year in which Huddersfield's choral society was formed; the Hereford society began a year later. The time had certainly come for Worcester to contribute in a similar way to the great English choral tradition, not only for local music making, but also to provide singers for the annual Three Choirs Festival, held in turn in the three cathedral cities of Worcester, Hereford and Gloucester. Whilst this history does not aim to cover the Three Choirs Festival, already in 1860 over a hundred years old, the festival must be recognized as of very considerable importance in inspiring Worcester's musicians, both professional and amateur, to found a new 'Festival' choral society in 1861.

William Done (Worcester Cathedral Library)

2

BEGINNINGS (1861-1868)

The name that appears in Worcester concert programmes for over fifty years is that of William Done (his name rhymes with 'stone'), and in his apparently quiet, unassuming way he must have had considerable influence in bringing together the musical traditions of City and Cathedral. Born in Worcester a few months after the Battle of Waterloo in 1815, he lived his eighty years in the city, becoming successively a Cathedral chorister, pupil-assistant to the organist, Charles Clarke, and, on Clarke's death in 1844, organist. He brought about considerable improvements in the Cathedral services, conducted well-rehearsed reliable performances at Three Choirs Festivals, and was the conductor at most of the city's concerts already described. He had the engaging hobby of keeping canaries housed in an aviary fitted up in the attic of the organist's house at 7 College Yard. Was it he, one wonders, who first suggested that Worcester should have an official choral society, and that from it should be drawn singers from his own city and county, instead of from choirs from distant towns, to form the chorus for Three Choirs Festival performances each year?

Two other Worcester citizens who may have discussed this with William Done were the brothers John and William Leicester, owners of a printing business in the High Street, four doors from the Elgar music shop. The sign for the Leicester premises can clearly be seen on the illustration on the next page. The Leicester family had a very long association with music-making in Worcester, with the Elgar family and with the Worcester Festival Choral Society. The Leicesters were staunch Roman

Worcester High Street and Cathedral (photograph Clive Haynes)

Catholics, and when the organist's post at St George's Church fell vacant, John (who sang in the Church choir) persuaded W H Elgar, with whom he had formed a friendship through their singing together in the Glee Club, to apply. W H Elgar, then a Protestant, was appointed and subsequently became a Roman Catholic. Hubert Leicester (1855-1939), son of John's brother William, became a close and life-long friend of Edward Elgar from the days when they went to school together at Littleton House. An accountant by profession, Hubert Leicester became head of his firm and the first Catholic Mayor of Worcester, an office he held five times. One of his interests was local history, and his book *Forgotten Worcester* (1930) has a Foreword by Edward Elgar.

Although there is no documentation to provide a precise answer as to exactly how Worcester Festival Choral Society (WFCS) was founded, it is certain from the first rule book that it dates from 1861, and from evidence in the Worcester Record Office that the first concert was held on 12 June 1862 in the Music Hall in the Cornmarket. This building, later known as the Public Hall, was to be the WFCS concert hall until 1939. It fell victim to developers in 1966, when it was demolished.

The first WFCS concert was held on 12 June 1862 in circumstances which might well have led the committee to think it would have to be postponed. The *Worcester Herald* for 14 June reports:

> The hall was completely filled with a fashionable audience, and the concert in its entirety passed off remarkably well. *The Creation*, first and second parts, was performed, in which the vocalists generally performed the solos very beautifully. The choruses, too, were admirably rendered, especially 'The Heavens are Telling'. Mr Tibbutt presided at the piano and Mr J Caldicott at the harmonium. Mr Done officiated as conductor on the occasion, with his well-known ability. Of course, the absence of the organ was severely felt: it was caused by damage from the storm of Monday, the rain and hail having penetrated the roof and unfortunately flooded the pipes. Happily this will be remedied before the next concert, and really it was scarcely possible to imagine the concert, crippled in this way, could have come off as charmingly as it did. We congratulate the society on its first night as a great success, and an omen for good.

An interesting note appears at the foot of the front page of the programme (illustrated on the next page) and of most of the others for the next six years, requesting that 'carriages, approaching the Hall, be driven down Mealcheapen Street, and retire by way of Silver Street or New Street; and after the concert fall in line along Silver Street. A body of policemen will be in attendance to enforce these regulations.'

Despite the flooded organ pipes, the Worcester Festival Choral Society's first performance had been very well received. This popularity continued: on 4 November in the same year, the *Worcester Herald* reports that 'the music hall was densely crowded' for a performance of *Acis and Galatea*, followed, in the second half, by a variety of solo songs, duets and trios. The reviewer judges most of the choruses as being 'beautifully done . . . especially 'Mourn all ye Muses'', but he pronounces the soloists' rendering of Handel 'not so happy'. The harmonium still had to be used, and this time 'Mr Elgar presided efficiently' at it, whilst 'Mr Done conducted with his usual steadiness'. The article ends as follows:

> We are requested to remind ladies who sit in the front ranks at concerts that the wearing of bonnets is not calculated to increase the comfort or enlarge the view of those who sit behind them.

There is a final note that the society considers giving 'an amateur concert' in aid of the Lancashire Relief Fund (already referred to).

This concert took place on 17 December, and is called, like those in the 1850s, a 'Grand Amateur Concert', with the WFCS named as participating. The word 'amateur', it would seem, was used for concerts organized for some specific purpose outside the performers' regular programme. Two surviving programmes of similar functions in the 1860s indicate a willingness to provide local, parochial help: a concert in 1864 was in aid of the restoration of Kempsey church, and one in 1868 for the new organ for St Clement's church in Worcester. The programme for the latter notes that 'the Festival Choral Society have kindly offered their valuable services.'

Meanwhile, the Society held regular concerts three times every season for the next few years, and the programmes reveal the continuing popularity of Handel. *Acis and Galatea, Judas Maccabaeus*, the *Dettingen Te Deum, Alexander's Feast* and *Samson* were all sung at least once between 1862 and 1868, whilst it was clearly

WORCESTER
Festival Choral Society.

FIRST CONCERT,

ON THURSDAY EVENING, JUNE 12, 1862,

AT THE

MUSIC HALL.

THE CREATION,
First and Second Parts.

PRINCIPAL VOCALISTS:

MADAME LOUISA VINNING.

MR. MASON. . . . MR. BRIGGS.

THE DOORS WILL BE OPENED AT SEVEN, AND THE CONCERT
COMMENCE AT EIGHT O'CLOCK.

PRICE THREE PENCE.

☞ *In order to prevent confusion, it is requested that CARRIAGES, approaching the Hall, be driven down MEALCHEAPEN STREET, and retire by way of SILVER STREET or NEW STREET; and after the Concert FALL IN LINE ALONG SILVER STREET.—A body of POLICEMEN will be in attendance to enforce these Regulations.*

LEICESTER AND SONS, PRINTERS, HIGH STREET, WORCESTER.

Programme for the first WFCS concert (Worcester Record Office)

accepted that *Messiah* must be given every year, usually in early January. In 1868, it was performed twice, once on 2 January and again on 28 December, this performance being referred to as 'an Extra Concert not included in the subscription series'. The choice of Haydn's *Creation,* Parts I & II, for the Society's first concert and the reappearance of the same work, or selections from it, would seem to award second place to Haydn, though no other of his works was attempted. The inclusion of Mendelssohn's *St Paul* (first performance Düsseldorf 1836), once in 1864 and again in 1868, reveals in William Done an unexpected willingness to introduce the work of a more recent composer whose genius he appreciated and whose music he thought his chorus could manage. The work did not appear in Three Choirs programmes for another nine years, and *Elijah* had not yet achieved the widespread acclaim that was soon to make it a staple of English choral societies' repertoire.

These oratorios normally formed Part I of the concert programmes, though sometimes in their place were cantatas of far less distinction. Locke's *Macbeth* was obviously still popular, as were Hatton's *Robin Hood* and Bennett's *The May Queen*. Part II was usually a medley of solos, vocal and instrumental, part songs, and, on several occasions a chorus performance of the popular Schumann's *Gypsy Life*. Sentimental ballads, glees, songs of Beethoven and Donizetti, selections from *William Tell*, the 'Bijou Song' from Gounod's *Faust:* they were all there in a glorious jumble. Modern critical appreciation may perhaps be too ready to scorn what it regards as tasteless and undiscriminating. Harold Watkins Shaw, writing about Three Choirs Festivals of the first half of the nineteenth century (ie two decades earlier), has this to say in his study, *The Three Choirs Festival:*

> As likely as not the true picture is not so much that Beethoven's Overture to *Fidelio* and extracts from *The Magic Flute* represented the taste of one section of the audience and Miss Cann's flute-playing and John Parry's 'recitations' that of another, but that the combination of these into one programme met the taste of the majority of the provincial audience of that age, which accepted them without a sense of incongruity. We should be wrong, in appraising these concerts, to offset one element against the other, and to regard the masterpieces of the Viennese School as instances of 'uplift' cunningly insinuated into a miscellaneous programme. Neither element could have survived so long side by side in such a case.

The Music Hall stage and organ (photograph, circa 1910, Clive Haynes)
The identity of the singers is not known.

The Music Hall: exterior of foyer on left (photograph circa 1880, Clive Haynes)

The first Worcester Festival Choral Society concert programme lists thirty-four trebles, as they were called, including Miss F Done, nineteen altos, including Miss A Done, nineteen tenors and twenty-six basses – a total of 98. William Done's elder daughter, Agnes, listed here among the altos, was a professional concert pianist, who appeared as a soloist in the Festivals of 1863 and 1866 and was rehearsal pianist to the Society. For the next few years the chorus numbers remained at about one hundred; in 1866 and 1868 twenty-five of these were tenors. It is not known how many of the singers were selected for the Three Choirs Festival chorus, but Harold Watkins Shaw writes of the second half of the nineteenth century:

> Even then the local chorus singers were submerged in the larger festival chorus, which continued to be recruited not only from the three local choral societies which began to emerge about that time, but from a large number of other centres. Northern choral societies, Lichfield, Birmingham and Cardiff were the chief sources of supply, but there was any amount of variation from year to year.

A beginning had been made; members of the new society had to compete for selection with experienced singers from the societies in the big cities, and even more, one suspects, with entrenched attitudes that insisted that the latter be invited. Moreover, any who were selected were gaining valuable experience which they were passing on to their fellow-members, even though, as accounts of nineteenth-century Festival performances reveal, works were often lamentably under-rehearsed, and on more than one occasion a chorus broke down and had to begin again. The remarkable photograph on the next page showing the oddly-placed chorus and orchestra of the 1863 Three Choirs Festival no doubt includes a number of early WFCS members.

For soloists for its concerts, the Society often seemed to be able to afford a soprano of some distinction, whilst the other parts were sung by Lay Clerks. For *Messiah* on 5 January 1865, the 'principal vocalists' were Miss Westbrook (of the Nobility London Concerts) and Messrs Hodges, Smith and Price of the Cathedral Choir. For the first time, the names of the instrumentalists appear in the programme: they include Mr Elgar (Edward's father) as principal second violin and Mr H Elgar among the violas. The principal violin is Mr R Blagrove, a member of another musical family well-known in the nineteenth century, and Mr H Blagrove leads the violas.

1863 Worcester Three Choirs Festival, showing, presumambly, some early WFCS members
(photograph and explanatory note courtesy E Wulstan Atkins)

The last Festival with the platform erected in front of the Nave side of the closed Choir Organ screen.
This screen was taken down in 1865, as part of the Lord Dudley's restoration of the Cathedral. Elgar,
who was 6 at the time was not present at the Festival, but he clearly remembered the noise and general
disturbance during the days of its erection.

The *Worcester Herald* begins its report of this performance by commenting on the well-filled hall and the success of 'The Worcester Band'. (It was known as the Band for many years.) The report continues: 'We have never seen the orchestra so occupied by a larger or more efficient chorus.' It then goes on to give that chorus 'no flattery, but very honest praise', and to commend particularly 'Oh thou that tellest'. Of the soloists Miss Westbrook from London is warmly praised, but of Mr Price it reported that 'he gave his music in a spirited manner, but we will recommend him to adhere more closely to the score of Handel'. He is especially reproved for taking a lower F sharp in 'and Kings to the brightness of their rising'. The report ends: 'A large portion of the audience customarily goes out early. This time before the final chorus, Mr Done stopped the music and saved the splendid chorus from being smothered . . . The arrangement was loudly cheered.'

The next concert of that year, *Judas Maccabaeus*, is not reported, but the programme note names another soprano soloist of the Nobility's Concerts, Miss Fanny Armitage, whilst the other soloists were Messrs Smith and Bennett of the Cathedral Choir. The report of the 1865 June concert states 'with the thermometer at such a height as it has been this week, a large audience was not expected, but the love of music being one of the prevailing passions in Worcester, the hall was tolerably well-filled.' The final observation is that 'Mr Done conducted with his usual steadiness.' Clearly the music critic on the *Worcester Herald* was an enthusiastic supporter of WFCS: another of his articles, for instance, refers to 'this admirable society' and 'a brilliant concert'. The programmes cost 3d and included all the words of oratorios, cantatas and solo songs.

The organ damaged in the 1862 storm was not replaced until early in 1868, as revealed in the programme for *St Paul* on 28 February, which states, 'The organ recently erected in the Music Hall will be used for the first time on this occasion.'

The Music (Public) Hall shortly before demolition (photograph Clive Haynes)

R U L E S

OF THE

WORCESTER

Festival Choral Society.

ESTABLISHED 1861.

PATRON,

THE LORD BISHOP OF THE DIOCESE.

PRESIDENT,

VERY REV. THE DEAN OF WORCESTER.

CONDUCTOR ...... W. DONE, ESQ.

HON. SEC. ...... REV. R. SARJEANT.

SECRETARY ...... MR. J. H. LEICESTER.

WORCESTER :

PRINTED BY LEICESTER AND SONS, HIGH STREET.

The 1861 WFCS Rule Book (Worcester Record Office)

3

RISE AND FALL

While concert programmes and contemporary reviews provide evidence of music making from 1862 onwards, the first documentary evidence of WFCS is a rule book, which provides firm evidence of the Society's origins in 1861. The title on the cover of this little primrose-coloured book, printed by Leicester and Sons, is 'Rules of the Worcester Festival Choral Society' and, underneath, the words 'Established 1861'. The cover is illustrated on the previous page.

The first rule states simply that the name shall be the Worcester Festival Choral Society, and the second is 'that the object of the Society be the cultivation of Choral Music, and the formation of a chorus fitted to take part in the Triennial Festivals'. The third and fourth rules are concerned with officers and committee: in addition to the Patron, Presidents and officers named on the cover, there are Vice-Presidents, a Treasurer, Librarian and two organists; and those officers are ex-officio committee members, joined by eight others, two from each voice section.

The next rule concerns subscriptions: members shall pay an entrance fee of 5/- (except females who shall pay 2/6d) and each member shall contribute an annual subscription of 2/- to be paid quarterly. Members of other Worcester music societies paid no subscription, and singers in the Cathedral Choir were honorary members. Rules 6, 7 and 8 are concerned with the routine responsibilities of the treasurer, secretary and librarian, and the last-named is to impose a fine of 2d per copy on anyone who borrows music and does not return it within a week. The next two rules refer to voting procedures, which are similar to those in any society, and Rule 11 is concerned with admissions, for which the Committee – theoretically at least – had responsibility.

> The Candidate shall be proposed and seconded after a rehearsal; he shall then be subjected to such tests of musical qualification as the Committee shall think fit to impose; and, being considered competent, shall be eligible for election by the Committee.

The next rule is interesting in that it provides for a training class and a qualified master whose duty is to train persons in elementary choral music. The wording of Rule 13 is of linguistic interest: it states that the Conductor's authority is 'unlimited and irresponsible'. One of the meanings of 'irresponsible' is 'not liable to be called to account: incapable of legal responsibility'.

Rule 14 lays down that practices are to be held at least once a week, and anyone coming a quarter of an hour late, or leaving early, is to be fined 2d. To miss a whole rehearsal, except through illness or any other valid cause notified to the secretary on or before that rehearsal, incurs a fine of 3d, and absence from a concert 1/-. Anyone with four consecutive absences from practices will cease to be a member. Standards are further upheld in Rule 16:

> A member refusing or neglecting to yield a due obedience to the Laws and Regulations of the Society, or being guilty of any impropriety of conduct at any rehearsal, concert or other meeting shall on the first occasion be admonished by a Member of the Committee; and on the second, shall be expelled from the Society.

Although William Done apparently held no formal academic qualifications, his profession and position as cathedral organist entitled him to be 'W. Done, Esq.', whereas the organist, Alfred Caldicott, trained in Leipzig, is merely 'Mr', as are all the rest of the officers and committee members, except those who are 'Rev'.

It is characteristic of this period that no women held any office – but then 'females', who accounted for more than half the singing membership, paid only half the full subscription. There is no indication in the Rules as to the respective duties of the Secretary and the Hon. Secretary; but the fact that the first two men to hold those offices were an Anglican clergyman (Rev R Sarjeant) and a devout Roman

Catholic (Mr J H Leicester) shows how the power of the love of music-making could transcend the sectarian attitudes of the times. The generous provision of two organists is possibly accounted for by the enthusiasm of both and the difficulty of preferring one to the other, but this, again, is mere speculation. Certainly Mr Caldicott and Mr Quarterman held the office jointly for at least eight years, and Mr Caldicott is also sometimes listed among the alto members of the chorus.

Other documents relating to this period of the Society's history include two reports with accompanying balance sheets, both of which were presented at the General Meeting held at the Guildhall in Worcester. The first of these is for the years 1865-6 and 1866-7, and the second is for 1868. Both are printed, as are the programmes of these years, by Eaton & Son of College Street, and the secretary is now Mr M Eaton, whilst the Rev. W Rayson has taken the Rev. R Sarjeant's place as Hon. Secretary. Listed among the officers is also the Conductor of the Elementary Class – Mr C Jones – and also listed are eight committee members and four Orchestral Stewards, one for each voice part, although, of course, those representing the sopranos and altos are both men. Perhaps these stewards had very little responsibility, as they are no longer named in the 1868 report.

The first of the two reports opens with the Committee's apology for a debt of £18 2s 4d, despite stringent economy, and they, therefore, suggest increasing the price of subscribers' tickets to 10/6d for the Gallery, 12/6d for the Area and 15/6d for reserved seats in the Area. These subscriptions are for two tickets for each concert, and are confidently recommended because the present prices are considerably below those of other towns.

Numbers are then reported: 143 subscribers, 90 vocalists, 18 instrumentalists. The report continues: 'Of the 90 vocalists it would appear that only 54 have paid the subscription . . . your Committee begs to suggest that, in future, the subscription being payable in advance, no tickets for the concerts shall be sent to members whose subscription is in arrear.'

The next two statements reveal some uneasiness in the relationship between chorus and conductor: there is dissatisfaction among the members because 'very few new works are brought out at concerts', whilst the Conductor gives his assurance that 'as many new works will be introduced as the powers of the Vocalists and Band will admit: at the same time a considerable improvement is necessary in the attendance at Rehearsals before the Conductor can undertake the responsibility of their performance.' One wonders what has happened to the system of fines set out in the book of rules a few years earlier. The report ends with a reference to the appreciation of the concerts shown by the subscribers' good attendance, and an exhortation to punctuality of attendance by members and, in general, to their promotion of the Society's interests.

The 1867-8 report begins by stating that the number of concert subscriptions has fallen from one hundred to sixty, presumably because of the increased cost. Next comes a statement that, with limited funds available, the committee did not feel at liberty to raise the class of concerts nor to spend more on soloists. The report continues, 'as the giving of concerts is not essentially the object of the Society, [the Committee] leave it to the General Meeting to decide whether the Society shall continue to give concerts at all, with so little encouragement of the public, or whether, by the early publication of the programme of the season and the principal singers to be engaged, upon condition that a certain number of subscribers are forthcoming, the class of concerts may not be raised to a higher standard.'

One of the main aims of the Society set out in Rule 2 of the Rule Book – 'the formation of a chorus fitted to take part in the Triennial [Three Choirs] Festivals' – may not have been achieved. The next paragraph of the report states decisively that the Committee believe that 'the rules of the Society need examination and revision, and they strongly advise the omission of the word 'Festival' from the name, and Rule 2 from the rules of the Society, in consequence of the hindrance it has proved to the success of the Society.' Most of the remainder of the report concerns the new organ which, it is interesting to note, was 'the property of the Society' . . .

> It is hoped that as soon as the Organ has been permanently secured for the use of this Society, and under its auspices for the use of the City, a Swell and Choir Organ may be added, for which the Society has the pipes, &c. already in their possession; but the cost of erection and action will have to be paid for from Subscriptions.

The final paragraph of the report complains of arrears in members' subscriptions, to an even greater extent than in the previous year, and expresses the hope that a revision of the rules would provide for dealing summarily with such defaulting, and that, in future, discipline shall be strictly maintained.

BALANCE SHEET FOR 1867-8.

	£.	s.	d.		£.	s.	d.
Subscriptions...............	90	4	0	Balance due to Treasurer......	13	19	10½
Entrance Fees	4	10	0	Engagements of Principals	26	17	6
Members' Subscriptions	3	18	0	Rent and Hire of Rooms......	31	15	0
Tickets sold for the Concerts ..	14	16	6	Printing and Advertising......	22	1	6
Books sold for the Concerts	5	19	6	Music and Hire of Music	7	18	0
By Balance.............	12	16	3½	Refreshments and Attendance..	7	18	10
				Carriage of Instruments	5	4	0
				Hire of Instruments..........	2	5	0
				Secretary's Salary...........	5	0	0
				Carpenter, &c.	3	6	4
				Postage, Carriage, &c.	1	1	3
				Insurance	1	14	6
				Sundries, including Collector ..	3	2	6
	£132	4	3½		£132	4	3½

WFCS Balance Sheet for 1867-8 (Worcester Cathedral Library)

After that July General Meeting, the only other concert in 1868 was the 'extra' *Messiah* on 28 December, and the word 'Festival' has indeed been dropped from the Society's name. It is clear from these two reports that the casual attitude of some members, revealed in irregular attendance and failure to pay subscriptions, was weakening the Society. There was dissatisfaction because William Done considered the chorus, and, it seems, the Band, unequal to the challenge of more demanding programmes (and some perhaps said the same of him): and one can well imagine the mutterings and the explicit complaints from a chorus resentful at not being adequately represented in the Three Choirs Festival.

For these reasons, the last full concert of the Society for over twenty years was held on 28 December 1868. It appears, however, that Mr Done did not give up without a struggle. On 5 December 1871 a programme announces, 'Mr Done's Grand Concert', and, underneath, 'the proceeds to be applied in discharge of certain liabilities of the Worcester Choral Society'. Inside is printed, 'Chorus: Mr Done's

Festival Choral Society.

CHRISTMAS PERFORMANCE

OF

"THE MESSIAH,"

AT THE

MUSIC HALL,

WORCESTER,

ON THURSDAY, JANUARY 2, 1868.

Principal Vocalists:

SOPRANO,

MRS. A. SUTTON.

ALTO,

MR. HODGES.

TENOR,

MESSRS. DYSON, PUGH, AND SMITH.

BASS,

MESSRS. MILLWARD AND PRICE.

LEADER . MR. SPRAY.

PIANO-FORTE . . . . MR. QUARTERMAN.

CONDUCTOR . MR. DONE.

The Doors will be open at Seven, and the Concert commence at Eight.

PRICE THREE-PENCE.

WFCS programme (Worcester Record Office)

Festival Chorus'. The works performed are hardly inspiring: Barnett's cantata *Paradise and the Peri* (first performance in Worcester) with a lamentable libretto; and a miscellany of vocal and instrumental works, including Mendelssohn's *Rondo Brillant* in E flat, and, yet again, Schumann's *Gypsy Life*.

It seems that during these years Mr Done formed a Festival Class (it is not referred to as the Choral Society Class), from which may have been selected some singers for the Three Choirs Festival; and it is possible that the members of that class were drawn from the Choral Society, which had last performed in 1868. The class was clearly appreciative of William Done's efforts, as in the Cathedral Music Library there is a somewhat ornate baton, bearing on its case an inscription 'Presented by the members of the Worcester Festival Class to William Done, as a mark of respect and esteem. May 1872'.

In 1873, there were two more Grand Concerts, the proceeds of which were not only to help reduce the Choral Society's debts, but also to contribute 'towards the purchase of a new pianoforte for the use of the Festival Class'. On 22 January the chorus sang Macfaren's *Christmas Cantata* as the Part I, and in Part II, Pearsall's *Purple Glows the Forest Mountains* [sic], Donizetti's *Rataplan* and one chorus from Hatton's *Robin Hood*. In addition, William Done performed a Handel organ concerto.

Part I of the second concert, in April, consisted of another work by Barnett – *The Ancient Mariner* – and this was followed by the usual miscellany in Part II, including *Sir Patrick Spens* ('by desire'). The back page of the programme is a full-page advertisement for 'Elgar Brothers' Foreign and English Pianoforte and Music Warehouse (by appointment to her late Majesty Queen Adelaide). Pianos, harmoniums, etc. 10 High Street'. An account book has a statement stuck on the inside back cover headed 'Balance of Mr Done's Festival Class Concerts for 1873', proving that his efforts met with some success, as a profit of £8 4s 9d is recorded, which includes a gift of £3 3s 0d from Earl Beauchamp and of the use of piano and harmonium from Messrs Elgar.

Edward Elgar, leader of the WFCS 'Band' in the 1890s
(courtesy Elgar Birthplace Trust)

4

A NEW BEGINNING (1887-1897)

After 1873 there is no record of the WFCS until 1887, when the name of the Society appears in the Worcester Three Choirs Festival programme. This must have been their first performance as the newly constituted WFCS, for all other references are to 1888. Material in the Worcester Record Office relating to the musical activities of the Leicester family provides the evidence: the archive that contains the 1861 Rule Book also contains a yellow booklet entitled 'Rules of Worcester Festival Choral Society', dated 1888.

Many of these rules are very similar to those of 1861, though the system of fines has been abandoned, apart from a 2d fine on the late return of music borrowed. The first rule gives the name of the Society, stating that it is under the patronage of the Dean and Chapter, that the Bishop is to be the ex-officio President; the Dean and Canons Residentiary Vice-Presidents, plus five others elected at the General Meeting. Other officers are the Conductor, the Organist (who is also the sub-conductor), Treasurer, Secretary (one only) and Librarian. The Committee consists of President, Vice-Presidents, officers and five others, representing the four voice parts and one from the 'Orchestral Branch'. The object of the Society is 'the Advancement of the knowledge and pursuit of music among members and the public by giving concerts, by rendering assistance in the musical portion of special services in the Cathedral, by taking part in the Chorus at the Triennial Musical Festivals and [other activities] determined by the Committee.'

The Conductor (William Done, now aged 73) is to select the music and engage the artistes, and must not exceed the sum voted by the Committee for the expense of each concert. There is an initial entrance fee of five shillings, and an annual subscription of the same amount to be paid in advance.

A new rule, on a slip of paper inserted, states that the instrumental members shall be bound by the same rules and pay the same subscription and entrance fee as the choral members. At this date WFCS had its own Band of orchestral players drawn from local musicians. Among these orchestral members were Edward Elgar and friends.

The 1888 Rule Book also states that absence from one-third of rehearsals debars a member from taking part in a performance, and absence from four consecutive rehearsals without valid cause leads to dismissal from the Society. An interesting rule appears near the end: for the special Cathedral services 'those only who have been baptized and are prepared to conform to the customs of the Cathedral' may take part. (It must be remembered, of course, that the Music Hall continued to be the venue for the regular concerts.)

In the same archive as the Rule Book is a printed slip dated 1893-4 (illustrated on the next page) which indicates that the officers were determined to make members observe the rules. It states: 'Members will oblige by paying their subscription for the current year to the Hon. Treasurer . . . not later than the 28th instant.' There is a forceful footnote: 'Your subscription for 1892-3 is also unpaid.' Human nature does not change! The Treasurer in 1887-8 was Hubert Leicester, a close friend of Elgar's. Leicester held the office for thirty years. The Rule Book, moreover, was printed by his family firm, Wm. Leicester.

That the WFCS founded in 1861 and the one reconstituted in 1888 were one and the same is confirmed not only by the two Rule Books of identical format and by the patronage of the Diocesan and Cathedral clergy, but by the first account book (also among the Leicester documents). The book contains the WFCS accounts from 1862 to 1868-9 and records from 1888 onwards; the book also includes the balance sheet of Mr Done's special concerts in 1873 .

For many years during the twentieth century it was believed that the Society was founded in 1870. This belief led to the so-called 'Centenary Concert' of 1970,

Festival Choral Society.

1893 - 4.

Members will oblige by paying their Subscription for the current year to the Honorary Treasurer (Mr. Hubert Leicester, 15, Foregate Street, Worcester,) not later than the 28th instant.

J. W. SOMERTON,

Hon. Acting Secretary.

August 1st, 1894.

Rule 10.—Members shall pay an entrance fee of Five Shillings and an annual subscription of Five Shillings, payable in advance at the beginning of each season.   The season shall begin on September 1st and end on May 31st.

Your Subscription for 1892-3 is also unpaid.

An overdue subscription note from the WFCS Treasurer (Worcester Record Office)

referred to later. One possible explanation as to how this misunderstanding arose is that on 27 May 1870 the Worcester Musical Society was established. In the Worcester City Library is a bound volume containing the Constitution and Rules of this Society and the programmes of all its concerts from 1872 to 1881. Its object is stated as 'the practice and performance of vocal and instrumental music' and the number of 'ordinary effective vocal members' is to be limited to 80. The first President was John Whitmore Isaac, Esq, the Vice-President William Done, the Hon. Conductor Alfred Caldicott and the Secretary Edward Spark, who appears as a committee member of the WFCS in the 1866-7 and 1868 reports. Clearly this is a differently constituted Society from the WFCS, which has the Bishop as its Patron and the Dean as President (1861 rules). The Worcester Musical Society programmes were, generally speaking, equally divided between choral and orchestral works; and the only time a chorus is specifically named is on a single programme, for 'Mr Spark's Concert', two years later than those in the bound volume, which refers to the 'Worcester Amateur Vocal Union'.

One can understand why confusion arose over the origins of WFCS. The Society appears to have foundered in 1868, and those who wanted to go on singing would have welcomed the opportunity to join the choral section of the Worcester Musical Society in 1870. Worcester's musicians, both professional and amateur, were a comparatively small number of people who took part with enthusiasm in the city's many musical activities. William Done, therefore, accepted the Vice-Presidency of the new Musical Society and a few years later became President; Alfred Caldicott, known to most of the singers as the organist of the WFCS up to two years previously, had also on at least one occasion (1867) conducted their concert.

Other musical societies in the city, moreover, were active in the 1870s and 1880s. The rehearsals of the Amateur Instrumental Society, for instance, were for some time directed by Alfred Caldicott, and the instrumentalists were trained by Edward Elgar, who then became their conductor when Caldicott left Worcester in 1882. Meanwhile, William Done appears to have formed the Worcester Philharmonic (not to be confused with the later Worcestershire Philharmonic Society conducted by Elgar), which performed choral as well as orchestral works, giving, for instance, *Messiah* in 1877. It might be noted, too, that in that same year the Music Society repeated *Paradise and the Peri* which had been given in Done's Grand Concert in 1871. Members of the Elgar family (including the young Edward) played in the orchestra for this 1877 concert. It is hardly surprising, therefore, that the memories of both performers and audiences of concerts in the 1870s and 1880s had difficulty in ascribing the right programmes to the right societies, and were still more confused when going back a further decade to the early years of WFCS.

The nine years following the reconstitution of the Society in 1887 must have been difficult in many ways. William Done was seventy-three and in such failing health that his assistant, Hugh Blair, appointed in 1886, was virtually the Cathedral organist from 1889. Hugh Blair could not have been a greater contrast to the steady, conscientious, reliable William Done. Born in 1864 in Worcester, he became a pupil of Done and then of G Macfarren and G M Garrett before winning, in 1883, an organ scholarship to Christ's College, Cambridge. It was not long after his return to Worcester and his taking over most of William Done's work that he found himself in charge of the 1893 Three Choirs Festival at Worcester, when he conducted the first performance of Bach's *B Minor Mass* ever given at Three Choirs. He is pictured on the next page standing on the left in the back row (Done is seated, wearing a top hat).

Clearly a gifted musician, with considerable talent as a composer, Blair appeared to lack the strength of character to support his gifts. There were charges of inadequate rehearsals for the Festivals, and his reputation as a heavy drinker was apparently well founded. The story of his being found insensible in the organ loft on Christmas morning 1897 may be apocryphal, but certainly earlier in that year, in the month of February, one of the patrons of the Society, Henry Dyke Acland (a Malvern bank manager) felt it necessary to address the chorus at their first rehearsal of Elgar's *King Olaf* because of their disapproval of both Elgar and Blair. Jerrold Northrop Moore's comment is 'Acland seems to have taken matters into his own hands at the first *Olaf* rehearsal in Worcester. Some of the choir disapproved of the drinking habits of their regular conductor, Hugh Blair; and some of them seemed bemused at being asked to sing music written by Mr Elgar, who was after all only the son of a High Street tradesman, who had been known to tune their pianos.' What Acland said in defence of the two musicians at that rehearsal is not known, but part of his letter acknowledging Elgar's gratitude reads:

Worcester Cathedral Choir
Hugh Blair (inset picture) and William Done (seated, centre)

I was quite determined that the Prophet should be honoured in his own country
... I really believe that these Worcester amateurs believe that they are giving
you a great treat by attending the practices – some of them, at any rate.
(Jerrold Northrop Moore: *Edward Elgar: Letters of a Lifetime*)

Whatever his faults, Hugh Blair must have had a frustrating time, doing the greater part of William Done's work for six years whilst the latter was still the official organist.

During the 1890s Edward Elgar was leader of the WFCS 'Band', and there were often other members of his family playing. The illustration from the programme for *The Black Knight* on page 35 shows William, his father, as joint leader of the second violins, and Frank (Edward's brother) playing the oboe. In the same year, in a letter to Dr Buck, Edward wrote, 'Blair and I are pulling together and making things lively here.' By September 1892 he had completed the vocal and piano score of *The Black Knight*, and in a letter to Novellos stated that 'the leading Society of this district (Worcester Festival Choral) [were] announcing the first performance of the work early in the year at their second concert.' On 18 April 1893, Elgar himself conducted the work, now fully orchestrated and dedicated to Hugh Blair, and with detailed programme notes written by the composer.

Elgar's dedication of the Black Knight to Hugh Blair
Detail from autograph score (courtesy British Library and Trinity College of Music)

Cover of the programme for the first performance of 'The Black Knight' on 18 April 1893
(Worcester Record Office)

❧ THE BAND. ☙

FIRST VIOLINS.
*Mr. E. Elgar } *Principals*
Mr. F. Ward }
Mr. J. Rees
*Mr. J. W. Austin
*Mr. A. Quarterman
*Rev. Canon Claughton
*Mr. W. Chinery
*Dr. Ehrke
*Mr. Baldwin
*Miss Hyde
*Miss Holloway

SECOND VIOLINS.
Mr. J. Syers } *Principals*
*Mr. W. Elgar }
Mr. E. W. Priestley
Mr. E. Harvey
*Mr. Grove
*Mr. Hopkins
*Mr. Jarman
*Miss March
*Miss Baylis

VIOLAS.
Mr. Geo. Roberts
Mr. W. Griffin
*Mr. A. Smith
*Mr. J. A. Smith
*Miss Webb

OBOES.
*Mr. F. Elgar
*Mr. L. Hadley

CLARINETS.
Mr. T. Pountney
*Mr. H. Wigley

BASS CLARINET.
Mr. Jno. Ward

BASSOONS.
Mr. A. Roberts
Mr. E. Edwin

HORNS.
Mr. A. Probin
Mr. W. Bennett
Mr. B. Crowe
Mr. T. Humphries

TRUMPETS.
Mr. W. Moore
*Mr. J. Gardner

TROMBONES.
Mr. F. Goddard
*Mr. G. H. Leach
Mr. Engleman

The WFCS Band and the Elgar family
Detail from the programme for the first performance
of 'The Black Knight' on 18 April 1893
(Worcester Record Office)

Elgar's humourous sketch of the Black Knight
(postcard to A J Jaeger, courtesy Elgar Birthplace Trust)

The bass soloist for *The Black Knight* was David Ffrangçon-Davies (father of Gwen Ffrangçon-Davies). The highly romantic text, a translation of Uhland's ballad 'Der Schwarze Ritter', today has little appeal, but the importance of the work lies in what Michael Kennedy has called 'its airy, dancing score', in which the ear catches the various Elgarian voices to be heard in the future - pastoral, 'Spanish-rhythmical', ceremonial. For the rest of the concert, Elgar returned to his place at the leader's desk.

In 1895, the Society sang Elgar's *Spanish Serenade*, and the following year (21 April 1896) Elgar conducted the first performance of his *Scenes from the Bavarian Highlands*, a suite of six songs inspired by various locations in Bavaria, with words by his wife Alice in imitation of local folk songs. This performance was given with piano accompaniment. In 1897, his *Imperial March* was heard in the first half of the concert in which scenes from *King Olaf* were given after the rehearsals already referred to.

Meanwhile William Done, too frail, apparently, to take part in any of these concerts, was at last able to enjoy a moment of glory in July 1894, when the robes of the degree of Doctor of Music were presented to him. The *Worcester Diocesan Magazine* records that this honorary degree was conferred on him as a result of petitions from two separate groups of people: first, Sir John Grove, Sir John Stainer and Sir Walter Parratt, and, second, the Bishops of Ely and Peterborough and the Dean of Worcester. 'It was the recognition, in a sense the reward, of unusually long, most faithful and efficient services.' In his response, Dr Done recalled that, 'in his early days the Cathedral was a miserably cold and dirty place, and the services nothing equal to what they were now. Thanks to their excellent Precentor, they had now one of the best services in the country.' A year later William Done was dead, and the WFCS concert on 21 January 1896 included Beethoven's *Elegy* 'in memory of the late Dr Done'.

The first concert after the reconstruction of the Society had included an ode composed by Hugh Blair 'as a tribute to the memory of the late A R Quarterman' (one of the Society's organists, it will be remembered, in the 1860s). Further elegiac reflections, though not with the same local associations, were implicit in the 1895 performance of *The Redemption* in the 'Grand Gounod Memorial Concert'. So, as the nineteenth century drew to its close, and Hugh Blair, after only two years as the official cathedral organist, was compelled in 1897 to resign his post and leave the city, the WFCS looked forward to the twentieth century under its new young conductor Ivor Atkins. Of the kind of music-making described in these early chapters, Harold Watkins Shaw writes:

> In their earlier years these kinds of musical society fulfilled a somewhat different function from now, and are a significant aspect of musico-social history. I should put a watershed in the years 1925-30. Time was when a great many of them over wide areas of the country (and there were some in quite small districts) represented about the only public face of music - and this enables us to be indulgent and understanding about those miscellaneous jumbles of programmes. Orchestrally, too, they drew on, and gave employment to, local talent, sometimes with local clans as nuclei like the Elgars of Worcester and the Fawcetts of the West Riding. Then, for the singers, they provided a leisure-time activity more significant than now, and therefore appealing more widely. And for many, before the establishment of local secondary education, who had no literary or intellectual interests or knowledge of the visual arts - superior artisans, small shopkeepers and the like - they furnished the only direct contact with one of the higher manifestation of the spirit of man.

> (Source: letter to the author, February 1995)

Ivor Atkins (Worcester Cathedral Library)

5

IVOR ATKINS – EARLY YEARS (1897-1919)

Ivor Atkins came to Worcester Cathedral as organist and choirmaster four years before the death of Queen Victoria in 1901, held the office for fifty-three years and died five months after the accession of Queen Elizabeth II in 1950. Because of this long time span this book covers the history of WFCS under the direction of Ivor Atkins in two chapters.

Born on the outskirts of Llandaff in November 1869, Ivor was the sixth of seven children of Frederick Atkins, a professional musician and for many years organist of St John's Church, Cardiff. First taught by his father, Ivor then had organ lessons from Charles Lee Williams, organist at Llandaff (and later at Gloucester). While still a boy he was organist at two Welsh churches, going on to his first professional organist's post at a church in Stonehaven, Scotland. Shortly afterwards he was invited by G R Sinclair to become his assistant at Truro, and when Sinclair moved to Hereford in 1889, he took his young assistant with him. The following year Ivor came with Sinclair to the Worcester Three Choirs Festival and wrote an account of his excitement at the whole experience, especially at seeing Elgar conduct his *Froissart* overture, a work in which Ivor was particularly interested as he had just been reading Froissart's Chronicles. 'I knew that Elgar was the man for me . . . I knew that I completely understood his music and that my heart and soul went with it.'

Whilst at Hereford, Ivor studied for his Mus Bac, which he took at Oxford in 1892; shortly afterwards he gained his FRCO. In 1893 he went to Ludlow as organist of St Lawrence's, but after four years he was invited to take Blair's place at Worcester. One can imagine his pleasure at this appointment and at receiving, even before he left Ludlow, a letter of congratulations from Elgar. Also in this letter was a query about the conductorship of WFCS. Elgar stated that he had conducted the orchestral branch for some years – 'to help Blair' – but that he had recently resigned, thinking that, as it is always understood that the cathedral organist is the Society's conductor, Ivor would want to continue that tradition. If, however, he did not want 'to be bothered with the Society', Elgar himself might apply, as he did not want an outsider to have it. 'I think there is great scope,' he concluded, 'for the formation of a big society in W. if 'worked up'.' Ivor Atkins replied that, if offered the conductorship of the Choral Society, he would decidedly accept it, but that, though he would welcome the experience of responsibility for the orchestral branch, he felt diffident about succeeding Elgar and would like him to continue. 'Please do not regard this as an idle act of courtesy,' is his conclusion, 'but weigh very carefully in your mind the musical experience of Worcester. I think I shall be able to bring a fair proportion of energy and enthusiasm to my work - but this is not all that is wanted.'

Finally, however, Ivor Atkins decided to take over both the choral and orchestral branches, and John W Austin, a professional violinist and a Worcester citizen, became leader of the orchestra. Meanwhile, Elgar had given up the honorary leadership of the Society, partly in order to concentrate on composing, but also because he wanted to form a separate society. Later that year, in fact, the Worcestershire Philharmonic was founded, two of its members (and later Vice-Presidents) being Sinclair and Atkins. Two years later, one of the first singing members, Dora Butler, was to marry Ivor Atkins. Their home for the rest of their lives was 8 College Yard in Worcester. There, their son and only child, Wulstan, grew up. Another frequent visitor was Ivor Atkins's closest friend and his son's godfather, Edward Elgar.

When Ivor Atkins took over the WFCS in 1897, there were about one hundred members, some of whom had that year taken part in the Three Choirs Festival at Hereford. At that festival, a small contingent of about forty singers from Leeds still aided the three local Festival Societies in the Festival Chorus, but at the 1900 Hereford Festival, Dr Sinclair felt able to dispense with the Leeds singers altogether and rely on a chorus drawn solely from the local Societies. Gloucester in 1901 also decided to rely on a local chorus. In 1902, Ivor Atkins was sufficiently confident to follow this practice, and from then on all the Festival Choruses have been drawn entirely from the three cities and their shires.

Wulstan Atkins has made the interesting observation that the Three Choirs Festival Chorus, and therefore the choruses of all three cities, came to develop a recognisably different quality of tone from that of the choirs from the big Northern and Midland cities, which had in the past provided many, if not most, of the chorus. This was presumably, therefore, the kind of 'western/Welsh Border' sound which Ivor Atkins's WFCS was producing and developing (see *The Musical Times* review on page 45). Certainly, the Festival experience of an increasing number of members was (and has continued to be) of great value to young and new members of the Society.

The organists whose names appear on WFCS programmes are Ivor Atkins's assistants. They followed each other during the early years of the century in quick succession: C Mason 1989-1900; E T Cook 1900-1906; E G Coombe 1906-1908; A Brent-Smith 1908-1912. The last-named, Alexander Brent-Smith, was a gifted musician about whose early days a pencilled note in Ivor Atkins's neat handwriting records: 'A E Brent-Smith entered Choir School Sept 15th 1900, left Choir School end of summer 1904, entered King's School Sept 1904, left 1908, with I.A.A. exclusively to Sept 1912. Studied Pianoforte, etc with me from moment of entering Choir School, continued with me at King's School and afterwards articled to me.' He was clearly proud of his pupil, who became his assistant at the age of nineteen, leaving four years later to become Director of Music at Lancing College. He composed a number of works in various forms, several of which were performed in WFCS concerts, as well as in Festivals (see the Appendix for 1912, 1924 and 1929).

In 1912, Edgar Day succeeded Brent-Smith, remaining in the post for half a century and gaining the affection of the Cathedral Choir and of WFCS members. When, a few years later, he was badly wounded in the leg in the Somme advance, the *Worcester Herald*, reporting a WFCS meeting, referred to 'the popular assistant organist who is in Epsom hospital'.

Worcester Festival Choral Society

UNDER THE PATRONAGE OF THE
DEAN AND CHAPTER AND THE
STEWARDS OF THE WORCESTER
MUSICAL FESTIVAL.

First Concert

Of the Season, 1904-5

IN THE
PUBLIC HALL,
WEDNESDAY, NOV. 9TH, 1904.

SIR EDWARD ELGAR'S

"Caractacus."

Leader - Mr. J. W. AUSTIN, Junr.

Conductors :

SIR EDWARD ELGAR,
MR. IVOR ATKINS.

EBENR. BAYLIS & SON, WORCESTER.

WFCS programme (courtesy Wulstan Atkins)

WORCESTER

FESTIVAL CHORAL SOCIETY.

———

PUBLIC HALL,

Tuesday, November 26th, 1912.

———

"We are the Music Makers"

SIR EDWARD ELGAR.

(First produced at the Birmingham Festival, Oct. 1st, 1912).

"Vorspiel and Liebestod"

Tristan and Isolde.   *WAGNER.*

"Hiawatha's Wedding Feast"

COLERIDGE TAYLOR.

In Memoriam, S. Coleridge Taylor, born 1875, died 1912.

———

SOLOISTS :

MISS SARA SILVERS.

MR. WILBER REED.

———

Leader of the Orchestra   –   –   MR. J. W. AUSTIN.

Hon. Conductor   –   –   –   –   MR. IVOR ATKINS.

———

BOOK OF WORDS, SIXPENCE.

WFCS programme (courtesy Wulstan Atkins)

The WFCS 'Band' became the 'orchestra' in 1901 and usually contained between forty and fifty players, sometimes including Edgar Day playing various percussion instruments. Throughout most of this period the joint leaders of the WFCS orchestra were J W Austin and A Quarterman; Hubert Leicester continued as Treasurer and Edward Spark as agent. The secretaries changed frequently: often two clergymen were cited as joint secretaries (Canons Catley and Wheeler and the Rev Manley Power all held the office), and when this was so a layman was listed as 'acting secretary'. Except for a few special Cathedral performances, concerts (two per season) were always in the Public Hall and usually on Tuesdays – never at the weekend. The programmes were beautifully printed by Ebenezer Baylis, contained all the words, including those of solo songs, and cost sixpence. A glance at the programmes listed in the Appendix reveals the surprising information that until December 1914 Ivor Atkins and WFCS never gave a performance of *Messiah*. The music of Handel, in fact, appears but rarely: there are two orchestral works, the F major *Organ Concerto* (1910) and a *Concerto Grosso* (1913): a solo song from *Acis and Galatea* (its popularity remarkably persistent) and in 1902 the one choral work – *Israel in Egypt*.

Throughout Ivor Atkins's conductorship shines his devotion to Elgar's music. Although those who sang in the Three Choirs Festivals had become familiar with *The Dream of Gerontius* from its first Worcester performance in 1902, conducted by the composer, the WFCS had to wait two decades or more before tackling it on their own. The main reason for this was almost certainly that the Society's funds were insufficient to pay for the many additional orchestral players that would have been needed. In 1903, however, Elgar conducted the Society's performance of *The Coronation Ode* in the same programme as Richard Strauss's *Sturmlied*. After this concert Elgar wrote to Ivor Atkins that the chorus 'did sing like Kings and Queens', and to Strauss that they 'sang well and had been well-trained and interested by Mr Atkins, ...[who] conducted with affection and the right spirit.' Two years later Elgar conducted *Caractacus,* and during this period the Society also sang *From the Bavarian Highlands*, *King Olaf*, *The Music Makers* and many of Elgar's part-songs.

A performance of Elgar's *First Symphony* in 1909 was enthusiastically received by an audience who filled every seat in the Worcester Public Hall (and therefore helped towards the cost of the orchestra, which nearly wrecked the Society's finances). At that same concert Sir Alexander Mackenzie conducted his *The Dream of Jubal.* Several other composers were invited to conduct their own works: Charles Lee Williams (*A Festival Hymn,* 1906), Horatio Parker (Professor of Music at Yale) whose *Come Away* was composed for and dedicated to the WFCS (1901), Walford Davies (*The Three Jovial Huntsmen,* 1902 and *Everyman,* 1905), and Hugh Blair (*Trafalgar,* 1905). Charles Villiers Stanford in 1908 conducted several of his own works, including *Songs of the Sea.*

In 1907 Ivor Atkins appeared as composer as well as conductor for a performance of his *Hymn of Faith,* the text for which consisted of selections from the Scriptures chosen by Elgar. A favourite work of Atkins's was Coleridge-Taylor's *Hiawatha,* and in 1900 the composer himself conducted *Hiawatha's Wedding Feast* and *The Death of Minnehaha.* This concert brought the special correspondent of *The Musical Times* down from London, and he wrote rapturously of the chorus:

> Its enthusiastic young conductor, Mr Ivor Atkins, to whom a thing of such fresh beauty seems indeed a joy, had taken exceeding pains (so many-tongued rumour wagged) to secure performances worthy of the works. Let us hasten to assure our readers that the chorus ... easily and magnificently beat the soloists and orchestra out of the field. We have heard many performances of the two cantatas, but can honestly affirm that the small, but most excellent [sic] Worcester Society was an easy first as regards those qualities which constitute good chorus singing - e.g. a good, round, 'musical' tone, crisp attack, and exact release, true intonation, clear enunciation, and an intelligent appreciation of the emotional side of the music in all its varying moods. These points are not brought out without much careful and systematic work by a thoroughly competent choir-trainer. ...The small chorus produced a beautiful tone; its quantity, however, was almost more astonishing than its quality, and it is evident that Mr Atkins has in these barely 100 voices one of the best and most workmanlike choral bodies in the Kingdom.

> (*The Musical Times*, 1 June 1900)

Ivor Atkins conducted this work on several subsequent occasions, and the programme for 26 November 1912 included a performance of the *Wedding Feast* as a memorial to the composer, who had died that year at the age of thirty-seven.

Samuel Coleridge-Taylor (Worcester Cathedral Library)

During these years up to the first World War, the greater part of the music was romantic. Several concert versions of parts of Wagner's operas testify to the powerful influence of the German Romantic tradition, which is heard, too, in lighter vein in Humperdinck's *Pilgrimage to Kevlaar* (performed twice). This is a setting of a poem by Heine, and the programme contains a translation of Heine's exposition, as well as a note by Elgar in which he actually compares Wagner and Humperdinck. Bruch's *Lay of the Bell*, a setting of a poem by Schiller, was also performed. Norse medieval history and legend are the inspiration, of course, for much of Grieg's music, and it is interesting that his *Recognition of Land* draws on the story of Olaf Trygvason, though he chooses a different part of it from Elgar. The works performed were mainly secular, though Mendelssohn's *St Paul* made an appearance, and Brahms's *German Requiem* was given in 1910. A subsequent favourite, Parry's *Blest Pair of Sirens*, was performed twice (1899 and 1912). A glance at the Appendix reveals that the miscellaneous type of programme maintained its popularity. If some of the music seems ephemeral and lacking in profundity, much of it was melodious, grateful to sing and to listen to. In the content of both music and words there is revealed a growing maturity.

When darkness fell at the outbreak of war in August 1914, the Three Choirs Festival, planned to take place in Worcester in a month's time, was first postponed, and then, when it was clear that the war would not be over by Christmas, cancelled. The WFCS must have decided sometime in September to cancel their usual autumn concert and instead to perform *Messiah* in December. Atkins wrote in the middle of October to tell Elgar that rehearsals had already begun (as they would have needed to, since the Society had apparently not sung the work since 1868). The Public Hall was not available for concerts, but 'by kind permission of Arthur Carlton' the Theatre Royal in Worcester (illustrated on the next page) was made available (some local readers may remember this theatre in Angel Street). The soloists gave their services and the programme announced that the performance was 'In aid of the Worcester Belgian Relief Fund', and that 'in view of this being a Sacred Performance it is requested that there shall be no applause'.

During those four war years, it is clear that Ivor Atkins and the Society's officers kept WFCS going, in however attenuated a form. In April 1915 there was in the

Theatre Royal, Angel Street (Clive Haynes)

Cathedral a performance of Bach's *Christmas Oratorio* (one is somewhat puzzled by the choice of work for the time of year), and the chorus consisted of 'Choral Societies from Colwall, Fownes (Worcester), St John's (Worcester), Wribbenhall, Astley, Bushley, Croome, Norton, Hagley, Pershore, Glenbrooke (West Malvern), Stoke Works, St George's (Redditch), Newland, Astwood Bank, Hartlebury, Kidderminster and the Worcester Festival Choral Society'. That some of the villages named could be listed as having a choral society is a matter for wonder; and interesting, too, is the mention of such groups in at least two factories – Fownes and Stoke Works. The explanation seems to lie in the existence of a Worcestershire Musical Competition, as in April of the following year there was a performance of Handel's *Samson* in the Cathedral, 'to be sung by Choirs of the Worcestershire Musical Competition', and there follows a list of those choirs, slightly fewer in number than a year earlier.

Early in 1917 when war casualties were appallingly heavy, it was decided that the largest memorial service yet held in the Cathedral should take place in March, and that Elgar's *For the Fallen* should be performed. Subscribers to WFCS volunteered to cover the expenses, which meant that a professional soprano could be engaged for the solo part, and that the whole of the offertory went to the Red Cross. One of Elgar's suggestions for the soloist – Carrie Tubb – was chosen, and the composer himself agreed to conduct. Wulstan Atkins, a twelve-year-old chorister at the time, remembers that service in remarkable detail. He recalls that Edgar Day was released from Epsom Hospital to be present and to play the organ for the National Anthem, and Wulstan writes: 'Keyed up as we all were, the performance in the evening - in a Cathedral which was packed as I have never before or since seen it - was the most moving and thrilling experience I have ever had. War conditions precluded the use of an orchestra, and my father had to fill in as much of the orchestral colour as possible from the organ. A special platform was erected over the choir steps for the sadly depleted WFCS ... The second stanza [of *For the Fallen*] begins 'Solemn the drums thrill', and I can still hear the roll of the King's School OTC drums.'

The emotional intensity that infuses so many recollections and accounts of the First World War is typified in his account of the rest of the service: the sounding of the Last Post; the singing of a Russian funeral anthem; his father playing the Prelude to *Gerontius;* the choir's singing of Bach's *Jesu, Priceless Treasure*; Carrie Tubb's *I know that my Redeemer Liveth*; the congregation's singing of 'O God our help in ages past'; and the final National Anthem. WFCS again joined the Cathedral Choir for yet another memorial service in March 1918, when they sang Cherubini's *Requiem;* and there was doubtless a final Armistice Service the following November.

The four terrible war years were finally over, and though so much and so many were gone, gradually WFCS – like societies and groups all over the country – was able to resume its full life.

Ivor Atkins (Worcester Cathedral Library)

6

IVOR ATKINS – LATER YEARS (1919 - 1950)

Towards the end of 1920, Ivor Atkins sat for and was awarded his doctorate, which he had always been determined to gain by examination, not as an honorary degree. A few months earlier, he had conducted in Worcester the first post-war Three Choirs Festival, and for his services to music in general and for his initiative in restoring the Festival after its seven-year lapse, he was awarded a knighthood in the New Year's Honours list. For him personally, therefore, the immediate post-war period was a rewarding one.

In December 1919 WFCS was again able to give a concert in the Public Hall, and *Messiah,* with perhaps a special appropriateness, was chosen. There was again printed in the programme the request for no applause. Out of the small chamber orchestra of twenty-three string players, fourteen were women; but Edgar Day was back and played the drums, whilst Dr H G Ley was the organist. On scanning the programmes for the next few years, one might imagine they are for the concerts of at least a decade before the war: there are *Hiawatha's Wedding Feast* and *the Death of Minnehaha,* the usual medley of solo songs, and Handel's *Acis and Galatea.* The last named was performed in 1920, a week after Ivor Atkins had been awarded his D Mus, and before the concert began the WFCS acting secretary, Mr W T Potter, presented their conductor with a silver cigarette box, referring to his determination to succeed by examination, and to 'his infinite capacity for detail and the great pains he took in rehearsal'. During the next few years there were Elgar's *Caractacus* (with an orchestra augmented by the Birmingham City Orchestra, including Paul Beard); his

Serenade for Strings, and his part songs 'My Love Dwelt in a Northern Land' and 'Death on the Hills'. Of the performance of these, Sir Ivor wrote to the composer, 'They sang them like poets . . . The finest piece of singing that has ever been heard in Worcester in my day . . . was that of 'Death on the Hills.''

Retrospective though these programmes seem to be, however, there are glimpses of new material: in 1921, for instance, a Purcell suite for strings and the Bach 8-part motet *Be not Afraid*, with which the programme opened. Printed underneath is 'the Motet will be repeated later in the programme, in order that the audience may be able to enter into and understand better the greatness of the work.' This admirable practice was repeated for two Holst works in 1923: two psalms and *Turn Back, O Man*; and for Bach's *Come, Jesu, Come* in 1927.

In 1922, at last, WFCS sang Bach's *B Minor Mass* for the first time. In a letter to Elgar Sir Ivor wrote: 'We are all very busy here upon the *B Minor Mass*. I've never done it and had a great desire to leave it on record that it had been done by our WFCS (on the ground that a really good Choral Society should at some time try conclusions [sic] with it). I think it will beat me, but I mean to have a good try for it and am putting on extra practices. Fortunately the whole Society will back my effort for they love it – but JSB has crammed a good deal in for the time at our disposal.'

What may well have beaten Sir Ivor was the balance of the choral resources at his disposal. The programme for that performance does not print the chorus names, but they are there in a March 1924 programme, and there are by this time 69 sopranos, 41 altos, 15 tenors and 26 basses.

For the next two-and-a-half years, apart from a *Messiah* performance in December 1922, programmes revert to part songs and often-performed cantatas. At the end of the March 1924 concert the audience were requested to join in the singing of the second verse of 'Jerusalem'. This is the year when the Society's first extant Minute Book begins, and it is clear that during this period, and for a decade and more to follow, there was continual anxiety about balancing the accounts, and therefore considerable caution about undertaking the performance of a big oratorio which might draw a smaller audience than a more 'popular' kind of concert. At the AGM in 1925, however, these conflicting interests were expressed, as the press report reveals: 'The committee felt that the miscellaneous programmes . . . while hardly giving the chorus an adequate opportunity for employing to the full their high musical capacity, had given great pleasure to, and had been very popular with, the Society's patrons, who had expressed their appreciation in very generous terms.'

During the next five years, there was certainly some moving away from the miscellanies: *Elijah* was given in 1925; Bach's *Christmas Oratorio* the following year (despite a member's protest at the choice of a religious work, when a secular one would be more to the public taste); *Carmen* (March 1927, with members' subscriptions raised from 7/6d to 10/6d to cover the cost of the orchestra) and at last, in March 1928, *The Dream of Gerontius.*

This performance took place in the cathedral, before a very big congregation, with a chorus of 163, joined by the cathedral choir, and with Steuart Wilson singing Gerontius. Readers familiar with Three Choirs history will know that, for many years, for cathedral performances, passages not conforming to Anglican theology had to be cut, and this was so even as late as this 1928 performance. The enthusiastic congregation was untroubled by such tampering, it seems. It is surprising to read, however, nearly seventy years later, when standards of behaviour are said to have declined, of the fears of the Chairman, Archdeacon James: 'He expressed his great satisfaction at the orderliness of the congregation during the entry and exit to the cathedral and during the whole time of the performance.' Being reasonably certain of a big congregation – even though they feared it might be a disorderly one – the committee had voted to donate surplus funds to the Infirmary, which therefore received £12 19s 8d (which would have been £30 more had exemption from entertainments tax been granted). In the light of the constant vigilance over expenditure, this spirit of generosity is heartening, but, sadly, short-lived; two years later, a suggestion of a similar donation was turned down.

The performance of *Tannhäuser* the following year, whilst very well received, drew attention to the inadequate acoustic of the Public Hall. At the AGM Sir Ivor supported a member who complained that, in the hall, the orchestra drowned the chorus. His indictment of the city's failure to provide a proper concert hall, fully reported in the local newspaper, has been echoed time and again: 'Some 30 or 35 years ago, when the Corporation had the opportunity to provide a proper concert hall, they neglected to take it, although they had the opportunity of providing a hall in

Worcester Festival Choral Society
And Members of the Cathedral Choir.

SEASON 1927-28.

President—THE LORD BISHOP OF WORCESTER.
Vice-Presidents—THE VERY REV. THE DEAN OF WORCESTER.
SIR EDWARD ELGAR, O.M., K.C.V.O.

" The Dream of Gerontius "
(Elgar)

IN WORCESTER CATHEDRAL
(Under the sanction of the Dean and Chapter),

ON TUESDAY, MARCH 13TH, 1928.

COMMENCING 7-30 P.M.   CARRIAGES 9-25 P.M.

All Proceeds, after defraying expenses, will be
given to the Worcester General Infirmary.

SOLOISTS :

Angel - -   MISS ETHEL BARKER.
Gerontius - MR. STEUART WILSON.
Priest -   MR. HAROLD WILLIAMS.

FULL ORCHESTRA AND CHORUS.

ORGANIST -   -   -   MR. EDGAR F. DAY.
LEADER OF ORCHESTRA -   -   MR. J. W. AUSTIN.
CONDUCTOR - SIR IVOR ATKINS, D.Mus.

Chairman of Committee—
THE VEN. ARCHDEACON JAMES,
The College, Worcester.

Hon. Sec. pro tem.—
F. R. W. AYLIFFE,
12, Camp Hill Road,
Worcester

WFCS programme (courtesy Wulstan Atkins)

Worcester Festival Choral Society
AND THE CATHEDRAL CHOIR.

SEASON, 1929 - 1930.

President	THE LORD BISHOP OF WORCESTER
Vice-Presidents	THE VERY REV. DEAN OF WORCESTER
	SIR EDWARD ELGAR, O.M. K.C.V.O.

"THE APOSTLES"

WILL BE GIVEN   *(Elgar)*

IN WORCESTER CATHEDRAL,
(under the sanction of the Dean and Chapter)

On THURSDAY, APRIL 10th, 1930
At 7-30 p.m.   Carriages 9-45 p.m.

SOLOISTS :

The Blessed Virgin	MISS JOAN ELWES.
Mary Magdalene	MISS MILLICENT RUSSELL.
St. John	MR. PERCY MANCHESTER.
St. Peter	MR. KEITH FALKNER.
Judas	MR. RICHARD WATSON.
Jesus	MR. ROY HENDERSON.

FULL ORCHESTRA AND CHORUS.

Organist	MR. EDGAR F. DAY.
Leader of Orchestra	MR. J. W. AUSTIN.

Conductor - - - SIR IVOR ATKINS, D. Mus.

WFCS programme (courtesy Wulstan Atkins)

which music would sound as composers intended it to sound. They [WFCS] had to bear the consequences because the Corporation of that time made that dreadful mistake.'

WFCS's first broadcast was by the BBC Midland Region of Elgar's *The Apostles* in April 1930, sung in the Cathedral. There can hardly have been a greater contrast than that between the Elgar oratorio and one of the works performed in December of the same year – Constant Lambert's *The Rio Grande*. The first concert performance of this work had been given in Manchester at a Hallé concert in December of the previous year and repeated in London the following day, so Worcester's performance, barely twelve months later, must have been among the earliest in the provinces. Wynne Tucker, who sang in it, recalls that 'it received such appreciation that we had to give an encore – something quite unknown.' The following year saw a broadcast performance of *Gerontius*, again held in the Cathedral, and with Steuart Wilson again as Gerontius. The financial loss on this performance, as on the *Rio Grande* concert, reflects mainly the grave economic depression of the period. Thanks to the committee and their vigilant accounting, however, by 1937 there was a healthy credit balance, and the following year the Society invested £50 in the Post Office Savings Bank. The balance was doubtless helped by the Social Evenings, the first of which was held in the Guildhall in 1934, and which by 1938 were referred to as 'The Annual Social and Whist Drive'. Another boost was given by exemption for the concerts from entertainment duty, finally achieved in 1935, after much negotiation with the Executive Committee of the Incorporated Society of Musicians. (Sadly the Glee Club, after meeting for 113 years, had to close in 1933 because of the imposition of Entertainment Tax.) As a result of this exemption, ticket prices were reduced to five shillings, three shillings and two shillings.

The 1930s then, despite the country's economic plight, were years of consolidation for the WFCS and of an increasing reputation as the wireless brought their sound to wider audiences. After the broadcasts of *The Apostles* and *Gerontius* at the beginning of the decade, there followed the BBC's transmission of Walford Davies's *Everyman* in 1935, with the City of Birmingham Orchestra, and, the following year, of Hamish MacCunn's *The Lay of the Last Minstrel* with the BBC

Orchestra. The pattern of two concerts a season (usually November and March) continued, so that there was as yet no tradition of a Christmas *Messiah*. There is an interesting Committee Minute for 1937 recording that when Sir Ivor suggested *Messiah* for the first concert, 'it was felt that this work would not receive the wholehearted support of the older members of the Society'. When put to the AGM, however, it was unanimously agreed upon, so that, on 30 November 1937, *Messiah* was performed for the first time since December 1922. A few days before this performance, a contingent of twenty-four singers from the Society had gone, by invitation, to join the Hereford Choral Society in a performance of *Gerontius* for their centenary celebrations.

The musical world, the City and Sir Ivor personally had suffered a great loss in February 1934 by the death of Sir Edward Elgar at the age of seventy-seven. His simple funeral at St Wulstan's RC Church, Little Malvern, was attended only by the family and a few intimate friends, including Sir Ivor, but five days later, on 2 March, the Cathedral was packed with people from every walk of life, many of whom had come by special trains laid on from London and elsewhere, for the National Memorial Service. This service has been fully and movingly described elsewhere (notably by Wulstan Atkins), so that all that must be recorded here is that, following Harold Williams's singing of 'Proficiscere anima Christiana de hoc Mundo', WFCS, joined by singers from Hereford and Gloucester, sang 'Go, in the name of Angels and Archangels' to the end of Part I of *Gerontius*. Astra Desmond sang 'My work is done', and 'Softly and gently dearly-ransomed soul', with the chorus joining in with 'Lord, thou hast been our refuge' and 'Praise to the Holiest'. After the Bishop's reading and two final prayers, the service closed with the last part of *The Kingdom*. Elsie Suddaby sang 'The Sun goeth down', followed by the choruses 'Our Father', 'Ye have received the Spirit of Adoption' and 'Thou, O Lord art our Father, our Redeemer, and we are thine'.

In 1938 John W Austin died. He had worked closely with Sir Ivor and Elgar in correcting proofs of the latter's works; Wulstan Atkins writes that in 1932 Elgar dedicated his *Serenade for Piano* to him 'as a token of appreciation of their long friendship and for his help in 'editing' over forty years . . . My father was delighted, for he shared Elgar's affection for a mutual friend.' John Austin's death, after leading

WORCESTER FESTIVAL CHORAL SOCIETY

SEASON – 1949-50

Tuesday, March 21st

at 7 p.m.

IN THE CATHEDRAL

(with the sanction of the Dean and Chapter)

THE CREATION

(Haydn)

Singers :
DOROTHY BOND
WILLIAM HERBERT
GORDON CLINTON

Leaders of Orchestra - - -	{ GEORGE STRATTON CECIL LAUBACH
Organist - - - - - -	EDGAR DAY
Conductor - - - - -	SIR IVOR ATKINS

Hon. Secretary :
MR. C. F. FLEXMAN,
82 SPETCHLEY ROAD,
WORCESTER.

Subscribers' Secretary :
MISS K. MAINWARING,
GREEN HILL, BATH ROAD,
WORCESTER.

WFCS programme (courtesy Wulstan Atkins)

the orchestra for forty years, hastened the fading out of this branch of the Society. Membership had been dwindling as bigger outside orchestras were employed for the broadcasts, and although Sir Ivor was reluctant to see the WFCS orchestra go, and persuaded them to continue for another year, wartime conditions finally led to their disbandment.

When the war came in September 1939, Sir Ivor (then aged almost seventy) and the committee decided that the Society should carry on. At first, rehearsals were held at 2.30pm on Saturdays, but part of the way through the war they reverted to Monday evenings at 7pm, despite the blackout. The Public Hall was used as a British restaurant, and it was doubtless the use of the Cathedral for all the Society's war-time concerts that led to the post-war abandonment of the Public Hall, as, since 1940, all the Society's regular performances have been in the Cathedral. The programmes planned for December 1939 and March 1940 were cancelled, but instead, that same March, a performance of *Messiah* was given in co-operation with various county choirs and under the auspices of the Worcester Competition Society, as in the First World War. Between then and the end of the war in 1945, Brahms's *Requiem,* Haydn's *Creation* (Part I), Verdi's *Requiem* and Handel's *Samson* were all performed with the same combination of singers. The Society was also twice asked by the Mayor to provide a summer concert as part of the city's provision for 'holidays at home', and Handel's *Judas Maccabaeus* and Mendelssohn's *Hymn of Praise* were presented, in addition to which Sir Ivor gave an organ recital. The highly-charged, emotive atmosphere of the 1914-18 war is noticeably absent from both the programmes presented and the Minutes recording the Society's activities. Members attended rehearsals in the blackout, caught buses and trains at times that were often difficult, and, moreover, the bank balance remained healthy whilst the membership increased considerably. After the end of hostilities, the first programme, on 18 December 1945, presented a discreet but appropriate reflection on the turmoil of the previous five years: Handel's *Israel in Egypt*, Haydn's *Te Deum* and Elgar's *For the Fallen*.

During Sir Ivor's remaining years as conductor the Society performed *The Music Makers*, which they had first performed in 1912 (see the interesting title for the work on the programme [page 43]). Sir Ivor's own motet *Behold I come quickly* was one of the items in a 1947 concert, and the following year came a 'first' for the Society: Bach's *St Matthew Passion*, in preparation for the festival that year, Sir Ivor's last at Worcester. His last WFCS performance, in March 1950, was Haydn's *The Creation*, which, again surprisingly, the Society appears never to have sung in its entirety (it may be remembered that the very first concert in 1862 consisted of Parts I & II). This post-war development from predominantly secular concerts to oratorios and cantatas was the result of the move from the Public Hall to the Cathedral. Moreover, the rising standards of the Three Choirs Festival demanded a familiarity with some of the staple works which could best be achieved by preparation beforehand in the choirs from which the festival chorus was drawn. It is a fitting tribute to Sir Ivor that, in the last five of his fifty-two years as WFCS conductor, he should be revealed as fostering the beginnings of this expansion and development.

During the last ten years or so of his conductorship, when the Cathedral began to be used – at first for particular occasions and then for all concerts – a controversy had arisen over payment for seats. In October 1938, for instance, it is recorded that, whilst the Chapter welcomes performances in the Cathedral, 'it holds strongly that a money payment ought not to be made a condition of admission to the Cathedral'. The Chapter recognized that that was done for the Three Choirs Festival, but felt unable to allow the same practice for the concerts. Despite the persuasive arguments of the WFCS Committee, the Dean and Chapter remained immovable throughout the period of the war. In 1940, for instance, for the *Messiah* performance during Passion week, the ruling was that not more than 360 seats should be reserved for subscribers, and the rest should be free. There was to be a collection in aid of the Red Cross, but even when the proceeds of a performance were going to a charity permission to charge for seats was refused. The same response came for every one of the war-time concerts. Discussions continued well into the 1950s, until it was finally agreed that ticket sales on the night of the performance must not take place in the Cathedral, but outside, which by an extension of meaning came in a short time to imply 'in the porch'. A number of seats was always to be free, and those seats until recently were the ones in the Lady Chapel. Meanwhile, throughout the whole of the first half of the century the Society had aimed to extend the list of its subscribers (more recently – as well as a hundred years ago – called Patrons). By their advance booking for each season, they not only ensured that there would be at least some people in the audience but provided some working capital at the beginning of each season, a very important factor in the financially difficult 1920s and 30s. The committee member's name which recurs time and again in this connection is that of Kitty Mainwaring. She took over the work of subscribers' secretary from Archdeacon Jones in 1929 when there were 92 subscribers; she continued for years to write literally hundreds of letters, a great many of which received no reply; and by the time she handed over to Joan Phillips in 1951 her efforts had raised the number to 206.

During this period of Sir Ivor's conductorship other members began a loyal and lengthy service as officers, which they continued for many years after Sir Ivor's retirement. Charles Flexman became Secretary in 1933, shared the work with another member (W H May) from 1936 till the end of the war, then continued alone until 1956, giving up then only because of an expected move from Worcester which never happened. Two years later he became Treasurer, an office he held until 1976.

Many other members of the Flexman family, of at least two generations, have sung in WFCS and served on the committee. Another member of very long standing was F R W Ayliffe (known to his friends as 'Fritz'), Secretary from 1923 till 1928 and a valued committee member until well into the 1960s when he audited the accounts.

Longevity and long service seem characteristic of Sir Ivor's WFCS. In 1938 the Minute Book records that Mr and Mrs Edgar Cook had that year celebrated their Diamond Wedding, and that they had been members for over sixty years. They were to receive a silver salver at the social to be held in January 1939. That the second half of the twentieth century appears to produce fewer members of such long standing is not to say, however, that 'there were giants in those days'. Rather, it is the result of a social trend, whereby far fewer people remain in the area of their upbringing for the whole, or the greater part, of their lives. This movement over the whole country has undoubted gains as well as losses, since incomers from other areas bring different experiences which can produce a more flexible approach. Moreover, as standards of performance rise, making regular auditions imperative, mere length of service proves by no means the best criterion for the selection of singers.

High standards of service over a long period are nowhere better exemplified than in Sir Ivor Atkins himself. To the 'fair proportion of energy and enthusiasm' that, as a young man he hoped to bring to his work, were added application, hard work, and meticulous attention to detail. He was precise in his instructions, punctilious in his care, for instance, over diction. Punctuality and discipline were very important: in rehearsals his watch was on his desk and at exactly 7.30 he picked up his baton and began. It is characteristic that in some of the concert programmes is the instruction, 'Interval: Ten Minutes Strictly'.

Of his discipline, Tom Pierce recalls memorable examples. During one rehearsal, which must have been, he thinks, for the men and boys only, Tom remembers passing a sweet to a boy aged about nine sitting in front of him. 'Stop', said Sir Ivor to the Choir. 'Come here, you two.' Tom continues: 'no name was given . . . just the pointed finger. Sir Ivor held his hand out. 'Give it to me – what you have in your mouth.' This we did. I was about 28, married some three years. 'You will stand by the wall until I call you!' ' There they stood, for what felt to Tom like twenty minutes, but he thinks was probably about ten.

Another of Tom's memories is of one of the basses with a very good, but also very loud, voice. 'He was often asked to leave', Tom recalls, 'in the middle of the rehearsal – not once or twice, either. 'Mr Evans, will you please go home. I've had enough of you tonight. 'Yes, Sir', Mr Evans would reply, and off he went. He never failed to be back the following Monday.'

Together with this strict discipline (which was also self-discipline), went an old-world courtesy. If the weather became very hot Sir Ivor would ask, 'Would any lady present mind if I removed my jacket?' On receiving no objections he would then proceed to do so, usually revealing the sleeves of an elegant silk shirt. On one of those hot nights his sartorial standards occasioned another reproof which Tom remembers. Several of the men turned up wearing short-sleeved shirts, which elicited the following: 'If you want to come here looking like pugilists, don't bother to come.' To the end of his days as conductor he always looked wonderfully healthy, with his white hair and pink complexion, and Wynne Tucker has recalled that, like many of his generation, he attributed his condition to his daily cold bath.

References to the works which Sir Ivor chose and conducted makes clear his interest in music of many different styles and traditions; and what Watkins Shaw has called 'his fine catholicity of taste' is nowhere better exemplified than in his two

1930 concerts: first Elgar's *The Apostles* and then Constant Lambert's *Rio Grande*. This interest in contemporary works and new compositions is revealed in Sir Ivor's thirteen Festival programmes during which he introduced thirty-seven first, or first English, performances. That the WFCS concerts were able to include so few of such works is undoubtedly due to the cost of preparing them, which would have been beyond the financial resources of the Society.

Sir Ivor's interest in words and language led him to produce, with Elgar, what is now the standard English language edition of Bach's *St Matthew Passion*; and he was responsible for the text in the parallel edition of the *St John Passion* and in various Bach cantatas, and for the emendations in the scriptural words sung in the Brahms *German Requiem*. A favourite work of his was Debussy's *The Blessed Damozel*. Realizing that Debussy had set the words of a French translation which was based on a better poem than that in use in the English version of the score, he did a considerable amount of work on fitting Rossetti's original, and more beautiful, words to Debussy's music.

Sir Ivor's scholarly interests led him to found the Cathedral Music Library. In 1916 his scheme was to convert a part of the Cathedral Treasury into a library for the Cathedral's music treasures, together with music by composers connected with the Cathedral, especially Elgar. Though this never developed quite as fully as he had hoped, he looked after it for many years, later becoming librarian of the whole Cathedral Library, a work he continued till his death in 1953. Another of his interests was plainsong, and almost every Saturday afternoon he went to Stanbrook Abbey to talk to Dame Laurentia, renowned throughout Europe for her knowledge of plainsong.

When Sir Ivor died in November 1953, WFCS sang at his funeral, as they had done at Elgar's memorial service nearly twenty years previously, 'Go in the name of Angels and Archangels.' Dean A W Davies, Dean Emeritus of Worcester, spoke of Sir Ivor's strong sense of duty, attention for the truth and for accuracy in detail. 'He had sometimes been unbending in the presence of his fellow men, but in the presence of God he was a humble and devout Christian man.'

His ashes are interred in Worcester Cathedral, below the Gerontius window.

David Willcocks (photograph Brendan Kerney, courtesy Donald Hunt)

7

DAVID WILLCOCKS (1950 - 1957)

David Willcocks came to Worcester as successor to Ivor Atkins in 1950. His early musical training was as a chorister at Westminster Abbey, where he won a scholarship to Clifton College, and he then became an organ scholar at King's College, Cambridge. He served with distinction in the war, gaining the Military Cross, and when peace came returned to King's College, where he was elected as a Fellow and also appointed Conductor of the Cambridge Philharmonic Society. His next appointment was as organist of Salisbury Cathedral, from where he came to Worcester.

His vigour and enthusiasm, and his lively wit, enabled him to draw out in rehearsals an always enjoyable best from his chorus. To those who remembered Sir Ivor asking permission to remove his jacket, nothing so clearly illustrates the difference between the generations of these two most courteous of men as David Willcocks asking on one occasion in rehearsal, 'Could anyone here lend me a belt to keep my trousers up?'

His first performance with WFCS was Bach's *B Minor Mass*, in which his scholarly and sensitive understanding and authority as a conductor were at once revealed. Writing in the *Worcester Evening News,* A T Shaw praised the conductor's penetrating insight and declared that 'his technique – a clear beat which inspires confidence and makes difficult things seem easy – is delightful.'

It is not surprising that during his seven years at Worcester the future conductor of the London Bach Choir gave two performances of the *B Minor Mass*, one of the *St*

WORCESTER FESTIVAL CHORAL SOCIETY

SEASON – 1950–51

WEDNESDAY, NOVEMBER 29th

AT 7 P.M.

IN THE CATHEDRAL

(with the sanction of the Dean and Chapter)

MASS IN B MINOR

(Bach)

Singers :

ELSIE MORISON

GRACE BODEY

WILLIAM HERBERT

RICHARD STANDEN

Leader of Orchestra – – – – – – –	CECIL LAUBACH
Organist – – – – – – – – –	EDGAR DAY
Continuo – – – – – –	Dr. HERBERT SUMSION
Conductor – – – – – –	DAVID WILLCOCKS

This Concert is supported by the Arts Council of Great Britain.

WFCS programme (courtesy Marjorie Potts)

John Passion and two of the *St Matthew Passion.* Of the last-named, Henry Sandon, recalling his days as a lay clerk, writes that his 'most exciting times were two performances of Bach's *St Matthew Passion*, in which I sang all the different characters such as Judas and the High Priest. I remember Eric Greene as the narrator and John Carol Case as Christus, and before the performance Eric Greene told us stories of singing with the Festival Chorus before the days of David Willcocks ... and of another occasion when things went wrong at the scene where the Christus sings of the clouds of heaven opening. At the greatest moment of chaos, the conductor of the day stopped the rehearsal and said to the Christus, Roy Henderson, 'you must try to get the picture in your mind – imagine the clouds opening and the angels.' Roy Henderson replied, 'B———-r the clouds of Heaven, . . . are you going to beat in four or eight?'' David Willcocks's 'clear beat which inspires confidence' certainly prevented any such confusion in *his* performances.

Henry Sandon continues, 'At 'my' two performances of the *Matthew* they used the newly reconditioned Handel organ as continuo and it was played by Meredith Davies; . . . [Those two performances] are among some of my great memories.'

During his seven years at Worcester, David Willcocks presented works by Mozart, Kodály, Holst, Vaughan Williams, Parry, and also the *Mass in C* by Julius Harrison, the Worcestershire composer. He gave three Elgar performances – one of *The Apostles* and two of *Gerontius,* and his masterly control was perhaps nowhere better revealed than in the fine judgement with which he always measured the accelerando in 'Praise to the Holiest'.

One of David Willcocks's choristers, John Langdon, now on the staff of the Royal Scottish Academy of Music and Drama in Glasgow, has a lively memory of a performance of Vaughan Williams's *Hodie.* Though the account, strictly speaking, is part of the annals of Three Choirs rather than WFCS, it may perhaps legitimately be quoted here.

As a chorister in 1954, I was part of the group that sang the biblical narrative in Vaughan Williams's Christmas work, *Hodie.* The text was assigned to boys' voices in unison, accompanied at a chamber organ by David Willcocks. For the most part the narrative was entirely separate from the orchestral and choral items, but occasionally, at the end of one of these recitatives co-ordination was necessary with the main forces under the

A T Shaw (photograph Brendan Kerney, courtesy Donald Hunt)

direction of VW himself. In retrospect I can see that David Willcocks was probably very nervous about what kind of beat VW would give, as he said to us: 'at this point the composer will start to conduct, but you are not to watch him. Keep your eyes on *me*.'

Elijah was sung in 1956 (the first performance since 1925) and writing (as he did for so many years) in the *Worcester Evening News,* A T Shaw expressed his enthusiasm for the 'magnificent performance' and for Mendelssohn's genius. 'Particular mention,' he continued, 'must be made of the distant choir, consisting of the Cathedral choristers and girls from the City of Worcester Grammar School for Girls, who sang the trio 'Lift Thine Eyes'.' Throughout his time in Worcester, David Willcocks did much to encourage schools and young people in the city to enjoy music. A year or two before the Girls' Grammar School sang in *Elijah,* he had invited the choirs of several schools to sing the ripieno in the *St Matthew Passion*, and it was at his suggestion that a morning concert for schools was given by the CBSO on the days when they were coming to Worcester for an afternoon rehearsal and evening WFCS concert. During this period, too, seats at one side of the nave for the Society's concerts were reserved at a reduced price for school parties, and ex-cathedral choristers were granted free membership of the Society until they left school.

Another suggestion of David Willcocks's became so much of an institution that it has been assumed to be a tradition of much longer standing. This was the annual December *Messiah,* and although musical taste is turning away from the singing of baroque works by big choruses, so far WFCS's Christmas *Messiah* continues to draw large and enthusiastic audiences. At Christmas, too, members of the Society took part with David Willcocks's Cathedral Choir in the Carol Service, and on Good Friday (sometimes on other days in Holy Week), in the *St Matthew Passion* or the *St John Passion.*

There were two special occasions in the 1950s, the first being the Coronation Concert on 5 June 1953, which the City's Coronation Committee had invited the Society to give. (The programme is in the Appendix.) Since 1900, there had been three previous coronations – those of Edward VII, George V and George VI. Apparently, there had been no suggestion of a special concert for any of these. The second special occasion was the service held on 2 June 1957, commemorating the

WORCESTER FESTIVAL CHORAL SOCIETY

WEDNESDAY, MARCH 27th, 1957

AT 7 P.M.

IN THE CATHEDRAL
(*with the sanction of the Dean and Chapter*)

"The Dream of Gerontius"

(*Elgar*)

Soloists:
NORMA PROCTER
WILLIAM HERBERT
SCOTT JOYNT

CITY OF BIRMINGHAM SYMPHONY ORCHESTRA
(*Leader:* NORRIS STANLEY)

Organist:
EDGAR DAY

Conductor:
DAVID WILLCOCKS

This performance is supported by the Arts Council of Great Britain.

WFCS programme (courtesy Marjorie Potts)

centenary of Elgar's birth and broadcast on the BBC Home Service. This quite simple service, with an address by the Bishop, the Right Reverend L M Charles-Edwards, included a performance by WFCS of 'The Spirit of the Lord' (from *The Apostles*), 'The Angel's Farewell' (sung by Norma Procter) and the Angelicals' 'Praise to the Holiest' (both from *Gerontius)* and the final hymn, with congregation, 'Praise to the Holiest'. David Willcocks and Edgar Day each played the organ, the former a few months before leaving Worcester for Cambridge, and Edgar Day (aged 71) at almost his last performance before retirement.

After the Worcester Three Choirs Festival of 1957, David Willcocks took up his new post as Director of Music at King's College, Cambridge. Twenty years later, many members of WFCS recalled his Coronation Concert when his knighthood was announced in the Silver Jubilee Honours List.

Douglas Guest (photograph Brendan Kerney, courtesy Donald Hunt)

8

DOUGLAS GUEST (1957 - 1963)

The early career of Douglas Guest seems to intertwine with that of David Willcocks. Both had been organ scholars at King's College, Cambridge: Douglas Guest, after studying at the Royal College of Music from 1933-5, went to King's in 1935, stayed until the war came four years later and was succeeded by David Willcocks. Douglas Guest then served six hard years in the Honorable Artillery Company, commanded a battery in the D Day assault force and was Mentioned in Despatches. Following four or five years, after the war, as Director of Music at Uppingham School, he went to Salisbury in 1950, succeeding David Willcocks as organist and Master of the Choristers and conductor of the Salisbury Music Society. During his time at Salisbury he was also Deputy Conductor of the Bournemouth Symphony Orchestra and conducted several London orchestras. For thirty-four years he was chairman of the National Youth Orchestra. In 1957, he succeeded David Willcocks at Worcester.

In a number of the big works that he conducted – Verdi's *Requiem*, Mendelssohn's *Elijah*, Bach's *B Minor Mass*, for instance – Dr Guest had the gift of drawing from his chorus in performance something extra, a depth or a subtlety that perhaps they had not always realized in rehearsal. In his first season he succeeded in removing the choir and orchestra to the West end of the Cathedral, and the result was acclaimed enthusiastically by both performers and audience. Writing of the Verdi *Requiem,* A T Shaw declared, 'Perhaps the most important thing to report . . . is that the placing of the choir and orchestra at the West end of the nave is well worth the trouble and expense involved. When the chorus sang from the choir steps much of the tone was lost, but now the singers are . . . heard to greater advantage. The impact of the *Requiem* was tremendous. It was Verdi at his best: full blooded, uninhibited, sincere, theatrical and very thrilling.' More details of this important change will be found in in the Very Rev R L P Milburn's account later in this chapter.

It was during Douglas Guest's time at Worcester that Harold Watkins Shaw published his edition of *Messiah,* about which John Langdon has written:

> 1960 was probably a very significant year in 'historically aware' performances of baroque and other music. In 1959 Watkins Shaw had published an edition of Handel's *Messiah* which confined itself to the composer's original scoring: strings, oboes, bassoon, trumpets, timps and continuo. Otherwise at that time performances were usually based to a greater or lesser extent on Mozart's re-scoring, which involved the full orchestra of his day. Watkins Shaw's edition 'took off' almost immediately and it is still regarded as the standard one thirty-five years later, whether modern instruments are involved or (more recently) 'period' instruments. While it cannot be denied that interest in original performance practice has played a part, it also seems that economics have had a role: *Messiah* is one of the cheapest works to mount, since even the woodwind can be dispensed with if necessary, since they never play independently of the strings.

Douglas Guest's last concert in March 1963 presented a work which WFCS had not tackled before – Berlioz's *The Childhood of Christ.* Performed also in the Worcester Three Choirs Festival later that year, it has not been given since, though Berlioz's voice has been heard in Festival performances of the *Grande Messe des Morts* and his *Te Deum,* and more recently, in WFCS's 1994 performance of his *Messe Solennelle.* There is always a sadness when a conductor leaves, but when Douglas Guest left after the 1963 Festival, the Society could also rejoice with him at his appointment as organist and Master of the Choristers at Westminster Abbey.

During Douglas Guest's time at Worcester, the Dean, the Very Rev R L P Milburn, was chairman of the Society, and, when possible, a singing member. WFCS is very pleased to have the following account of his memories of that time.

> When I arrived at Worcester in 1957, I found that the conventions attaching to the concerts were more akin to an occasion when dignity prevailed than to a

popular concert of secular character. No applause was customary and the practice which I inherited without questioning it was for me, at the start of each concert, to ascend the pulpit and then to deliver a short but, as I hoped, relevant prayer, acknowledging God as the author and guide of all artistic expression. At the end of the concert I was expected to walk up in silence and congratulate the conductor. Whereat the orchestra began to disperse, followed by members of the audience. This convention was accepted by most as perfectly appropriate, but there were those who favoured the idea of more general applause and, just after my time at Worcester, a dazzling performance of *Belshazzar's Feast*, conducted by Christopher Robinson, led to a spontaneous outburst. Debate followed, and the views of respective Cathedral Chapters were canvassed with the result that, after a year or two of hesitation, applause at the end of each concert became customary. No doubt this corresponds with the conventions of the times but it came as something of a surprise to me when I returned to Worcestershire and to the concerts after an absence of a dozen years to see, at the end of the *Messiah,* a blonde Swedish soprano darting in and out to acknowledge a volley of clapping.[1]

Another question on which divided views were possible concerned the placing of the chorus. At first its members were normally ranged at the east end of the nave, but Douglas Guest, on his arrival two or three months before myself, urged the Committee to avoid 'seating the chorus in a way which did not allow the full volume of sound to be heard since chorus members on the wings of the platform were singing into the tower pillars.' It was explained that a tubular steel scaffolding platform, 'twenty-five feet forward of the normal position' could be erected for thirty-five pounds by a professional firm, and the Chapter agreed to the experiment for the next performance. At a committee meeting shortly

---

[1]Dr Eric Kemp, also a former Dean of Worcester and a singing member of WFCS, writes about the applause controversy at the Worcester Three Choirs Festival in 1969:

The first concert of the Festival on the Sunday evening was given by the National Youth Orchestra. It began with the the Brahms *Academic Festival Overture* and, at the end of that, I sensed a somewhat uneasy feeling in the audience. The second item was a Haydn trumpet concerto played brilliantly by an 18 year-old youth. At the end of that, the conductor leaned forward towards the soloist and very gently put his hands together in a silent clapping. This led immediately to an outburst of applause from the whole audience and they applauded to the end of the programme. The next morning I was beseiged by people urging me to stop this thing that had happened which, in their view was so terrible. I decided to do nothing but to leave the audience to work out its own solution. . . . The following year the Festival was at Hereford and the then Dean of Hereford, in his sermon at the opening service, actually preached against applause at Cathedral concerts. In spite of that, however, there was applause at the evening concert, applause led in fact by the Worcester contingent, and to the best of my knowledge applause has continued at the Three Choirs Festival ever since.

afterwards Douglas expressed high satisfaction, although I note from the Minutes that I felt some concern at the time – Monday to Friday – taken in erecting and dismantling the platform, which caused a certain amount of disturbance in the normal routine of the Cathedral. Douglas had an immediate answer based on changes which he had initiated at Salisbury – place the seating for the chorus at the west end, with the audience turned round to face them. And so a convention became established which lasted for a number of years – perhaps there is no completely ideal solution which combines the great and widespread happiness of the concerts with cautious regard for the fabric and the other activities of the Cathedral.

And 'widespread happiness' I found to be no exaggeration. I was impressed immediately by the enthusiasm presented by members of the chorus, fluctuating slightly in number from year to year but usually about 250. Fortunate throughout in the inspiration given by successive conductors, the chorus presented an attractive and alert appearance which usually presaged a splendid performance. I cannot imagine what happened shortly before February 25, 1957 when the Committee noted that 'complaint had been received from Patrons regarding the dress of certain members of the chorus on the platform'. Exception had been taken to the 'display of highly coloured hats and scarves by some of the ladies and the wearing of overcoats of various colours by some of the gentlemen.'

No such laxity prevailed at any concert which I attended, and in three or four of these I took my place as a member of the chorus. But, finding it difficult to attend an adequate number of rehearsals, I returned to the audience, not before I had enjoyed singing tenor in such masterpieces as Brahms's *Requiem* where my confidence was increased by my position next to Neville Dilks, a King's School master and lay clerk, whose rendering of the piece was flawless.

I found the Committee Meetings, at which I was usually asked to preside, agreeable occasions. The Chapter House, with its historical associations, was the right place in which to discuss music for today and tomorrow. A few members urged the claim of modern pieces, such as regularly found their place at the Three Choirs, nor were the conductors unsympathetic, but the only work in that class which could be sure of an enthusiastic, popular reception was Britten's *War Requiem*, and here the technical difficulties were formidable.

The question of finance was nearly always to the fore at Committee Meetings. Thus, in March 1964, Charles Flexman, the ever-vigilant treasurer, thought there would be an approximate loss of £850 on the season, against which could be set the valuable assistance given by the Arts Council of Great Britain, £450 that year. But by a series of well-judged balancing-acts the hazards were overcome. One of the most successful efforts was that proposed by Wynne Tucker, who succeeded Anthony Hayward as another most efficient secretary. Her idea of a 'Bring and Buy Sale' for capital purposes was, after the

The staging at the west end of the Cathedral
(WFCS under the direction of Donald Hunt in 1986, photograph Roderick Attwood)

WORCESTER CATHEDRAL

(with the sanction of the Dean and Chapter)

MONDAY, 4th MARCH, 1963

AT 7.30 P.M.

THE CHILDHOOD OF CHRIST

(Berlioz)

Soloists:

HEATHER HARPER	GERALD ENGLISH
JOHN CAROL CASE	JOHN SHIRLEY QUIRK

WORCESTER FESTIVAL CHORAL SOCIETY

AND

THE CITY OF BIRMINGHAM SYMPHONY ORCHESTRA
(Leader: MEYER STOLOW)

Conductor: **DOUGLAS GUEST**

The National Federation of Music Societies, to which this Society
is affiliated, supports this Concert with funds provided by the
Arts Council of Great Britain

WFCS programme (courtesy Marjorie Potts)

customary hesitations, readily adopted, under the rather more impressive title 'Sale of Treasures'. This proved to be a great success. Some who were unwilling to part with treasures made a donation instead and over £700 was raised.

But, as the old proverb states: 'It is the men and not the walls that make the city.' The remark has again and again been offered that the Festival Choral Society has been triumphantly fortunate in its conductors. The long and formative reign of Sir Ivor Atkins was succeeded by the years of David Willcocks, Douglas Guest and Christopher Robinson, each contributing something of his own charisma to a receptive and enthusiastic body of singers, all of whom would agree, with Milton, that 'such sweet compulsion doth in music lie'. Moreover each of the conductors found himself able to maintain a happy relationship with the City of Birmingham Symphony Orchestra, who were usually chosen to provide singers with the necessary support. Nor must Edgar Day's contribution be overlooked. The title 'Sub-Conductor, Accompanist and Orchestral Secretary' conferred by Ivor Atkins has a somewhat grandiose sound whereas Edgar's service to the Society lay in delicate and devoted musicianship extended over half a century. When Harry Bramma took his place there was a welcome for an access of new vigour appreciated by both the Choral Society and the Voluntary Choir.

In September 1968 the time had nearly arrived for me to move away to London. Margery and I were courteously invited to present ourselves before the Committee at whose hands we received a generous cheque and some treasured Worcester plates - 'coronet pattern'. We walked home in sombre mood, more than doubtful whether we were not being foolish in leaving so attractive a place as Worcester and such agreeable companions as the members of the Festival Choral Society.

RLPM.

Christopher Robinson (courtesy Three Choirs Festival Committee)

9

CHRISTOPHER ROBINSON (1962 - 1974)

In Douglas Guest's last year, Edgar Day retired after fifty-two years as assistant organist and conductor. He had played and rehearsed *Gerontius* under Elgar himself, and he played and rehearsed it for the last concert of his final season. His splendid service was marked by the presentation of a cheque and the Society's warmest good wishes.

Edgar Day's successor, Christopher Robinson, had received his early musical education in Worcestershire as a chorister at St Michael's, Tenbury, from where he proceeded to Rugby and to Christ Church, Oxford, followed by three years in the music department at Oundle School. After his year as assistant, he succeeded Douglas Guest as organist in 1963. Despite a keen interest in cricket (he is a member of MCC) it is unlikely that he found much time to visit the Worcester County cricket ground. He has provided us with this recollection of his years in Worcester:

> WFCS was very much at the centre of my life during twelve happy years in Worcester. I spent the first year as assistant to Douglas Guest, at whose feet I sat (almost literally) on Monday evenings in the Chapter House. I remember with much amusement some of his *bons mots* usually uttered in a sufficiently discreet *sotto voce* to avoid reaching sensitive ears. When I became Cathedral Organist I had the advantage of being known to members of the Society, and though some may rightly have been suspicious of my limited experience, the general feeling of loyalty and friendliness was overwhelming. Despite my occasional indiscretions this happy state of affairs seemed to continue. In my early years concerts were held on a Tuesday, and a full rehearsal with chorus and orchestra was not possible. I often wonder how we had the nerve to perform works like

The Kingdom and *Belshshazzar's Feast* under these conditions. It was always cold. Members of the CBSO clustered around the Gurney stove in the Cathedral wearing mittens and with their teeth chattering almost audibly.

I remember with particular pleasure the centenary concert (incorrectly timed, it seems) and others, which latterly took place on Saturdays, including such works as the Verdi *Four Sacred Pieces*, Holst's *Hymn of Jesus* and Britten's *War Requiem*. The standard of performance was often high, and it was sometimes easier to achieve a degree of unanimity than in the demanding atmosphere of Festival Week.

The Society had a wide age range. There were those who had sung under Elgar (of whom I was considerably in awe) and there was a large number of members from Worcester schools, some of whom have distinguished themselves in the musical world. Organisation was always smooth and efficient. I remember with particular gratitude the work of Winifred Tucker and Charles Flexman, and various chairmen, from the inimitable Dean Milburn onwards.

In 1962, Anthony Hayward resigned as Secretary having served not only as an extremely capable Secretary but, on occasion when the assistant organist was away, as a skilled accompanist. He was succeeded by Wynne Tucker, the first woman to hold the office, who gave distinguished service for fourteen years. There were other 'firsts' during the 1960s, one of which was the use of the Watkins Shaw edition of *Messiah*. For the first time, too, members of the Society, together with contingents from Hereford and Gloucester, began to perform in other cities: Swansea (1965 – Britten's *War Requiem*); Dudley (1966 – *Gerontius*); Royal Festival Hall (1970 – Jonathan Harvey's *Ludus Amoris*). In October 1970, the Society alone (ie without contingents from the other two choirs) was invited by the CBSO to perform Beethoven's *Mass in C* in Birmingham Town Hall, conducted by Maurice Handford. Yet another 'first' was the Society's performance of Bruckner's *Mass in F Minor*, in March 1967.

Christopher Robinson has referred to Tuesday as the traditional day for concerts. As previous chapters indicate, this was a legacy from the Society's earlier days, when singers were either free or, without much difficulty, able to be freed, for the final afternoon rehearsal. By the 1960s, only a very sparse chorus attendance was possible on a Tuesday afternoon, so that the conductor's final rehearsal with the CBSO, or other orchestra, gave him no indication of the balance of his forces and the chorus no experience of the orchestral sound. Worcester, the Faithful City, is slow to change its traditional ways, and it was not until 1972 that Christopher Robinson's proposal to hold concerts on a Saturday was accepted. It is hard now to realize that Haydn's *Creation* (November 1972), Britten's *War Requiem* (March 1973) and Monteverdi's *Vespers* (November 1973) were the first to be accorded the full Saturday treatment. About this time, too, the comfort of both performers and audience was much improved by the installation of the Cathedral central heating system, so that warm boots, woollen shawls, extra sweaters and the orchestra's mittens gradually ceased to be considered essential equipment.

At the beginning of the 1960s, chorus numbers were about 225, rising by the end of the decade to 290, and it is worth recording that in 1969 there were 33 tenors. Among these tenors was Don Parker, to whom reference is made below, and who had sung for more than half a century until his resignation due to illness in 1974. Fritz Ayliffe, who has been mentioned as secretary in the 1920s, celebrated his ninetieth birthday in 1966, receiving from the Society a present of sherry and champagne to mark the occasion. Having joined the Society in 1892, he continued to audit the accounts – most efficiently – until 1967. He died in 1969.

It would be most misleading to give the impression of a Society of old people, the age-range being, as ever, very wide. Mention has been made of the encouragement by David Willcocks of young people from the schools, and, as Christopher Robinson has indicated, there continued to be a number of gifted young musicians, several of whom, as well as singing, made generous contributions on piano and organ. On the few occasions when the assistant organist was absent, they accompanied for rehearsals. John Langdon, as a schoolboy, played the organ continuo for the *B Minor Mass* in 1961; in 1966, Stephen and Nicholas Cleobury and Roger Parkes gave an organ recital in aid of the Society's funds; in 1971, Stephen Darlington and Andrew Millington accompanied Rossini's *Petite Messe Solennelle* on two pianos. Some of these musicians have recalled their days with WFCS.

Stephen Cleobury succeeded David Willcocks as organist and master of the choristers at King's College, Cambridge. In 1993, succeeding Dr George Guest, Christopher Robinson, Stephen's one-time master, became his neighbour as organist and master of the choristers at St John's. One wonders how far the sounds of their respective choirs, traditionally so different, continue to diverge.

Stephen Cleobury writes:

WFCS had and continues to have a profound influence on both my personal and professional life. In 1964, recently 'retired' from the Cathedral Choir, I was encouraged by Christopher Robinson to join the Choral Society (and a joint King's School [boys only]/Alice Ottley [girls only] choir which he conducted). Although I enjoyed getting back to singing again it soon became clear that the presence of Penny (née Holloway) in both groups was an additional incentive to my attendance. We were married in the Cathedral in 1971, supported by the good wishes of the many friends we had made in Worcester Festival Choral Society.

Among the formative musical experiences in my early life, the introduction to the great choral works which I experienced through the WFCS and the Three Choirs Festival was highly significant. (I remember the competition there was among choristers to obtain autographs at the festival: my biggest catch was Zoltán Kodály.) I particularly remember the *Four Sacred Pieces* of Verdi having a powerful effect on me, and now that I find myself conducting this repertoire I have reason to be grateful for the insights I gained into these works through the training and teaching of Douglas Guest, Edgar Day, Christopher Robinson and Harry Bramma. Penny and I remember those days with great affection.

Andrew Millington, now organist and Master of the choristers at Guildford Cathedral, also provides us with recollections of WFCS in the days of Christopher Robinson:

My first impressions of the repertoire of large choral works were gained as schoolboy member of the bass section in Worcester Festival Choral Society between 1968 and 1971. As an aspiring conductor, I had no better initiation than to get to know the music from within the ranks. This was a rich experience for me and for several of my contemporaries also to become professional musicians. My first *Messiah* was daunting, in that it was performed on a minumum of rehearsal, assuming that most of the choir knew it extremely well.

The music of Elgar has a special place in the hearts of Worcester folk, and I recall a most moving performance of *The Music Makers* at the Society's 'centenary' concert in 1970, conducted by Sir Adrian Boult. We were indeed fortunate to work under the inspiring leadership of Christopher Robinson at that time, covering a broad and interesting repertoire. Choral singing is at the centre of local music-making and WFCS has made an immense contribution to musical life in the Worcester area over the years. Long may it flourish in the future.

WORCESTER CATHEDRAL

(with the sanction of the Dean and Chapter)

WORCESTER FESTIVAL CHORAL SOCIETY

and

THE CITY OF BIRMINGHAM SYMPHONY ORCHESTRA

(Leader: JOHN GEORGIADIS)

TUESDAY, 12th NOVEMBER, 1963

at 7.30 p.m.

MASS No. 3 (The Nelson)
(Haydn)

FIVE MYSTICAL SONGS
(Vaughan Williams)

Soloists:

ELIZABETH HARWOOD　　**ELIZABETH BUTLER**

PHILIP TODD　　**BRYAN DRAKE**

Conductor: **CHRISTOPHER ROBINSON**

The National Federation of Music Societies, to which this Society
is affiliated, supports this Concert with funds provided by the
Arts Council of Great Britain

WFCS programme (courtesy Marjorie Potts)

Stephen Darlington is now organist and master of the choristers at Christ Church, Oxford. He writes:

> I feel very fortunate indeed to have had the opportunity to sing in the WFCS whilst in my last four years at school (1969-71). It is not difficult to recall the thrill of participating in the great choral masterpieces for the first time, and in such an historic location. It is always true of the best choirs that the whole is greater than the sum of its parts, and it was certainly the case then! I well remember an elderly member of the choir telling me to get my hair cut, since it was so long he could not see the beat! With this, and other more plausible excuses to deal with, it is astonishing how our conductor, Christopher Robinson, produced such fine results. It was only subsequently that I fully appreciated the choir's good fortune in having a conductor who combined considerable technical accomplishment with a deep sense of musicality, and the ability to coax his singers into achieving a corporate musical experience, well beyond their expertise. This perpetuation of a great musical tradition is central to the existence of the WFCS. Long may it continue.

When Christopher Robinson became organist, his place as assistant was taken by Harry Bramma, who gave excellent service until he left in 1975 to become organist of Southwark Cathedral. In the early summer of 1963 both he and Christopher Robinson gave organ recitals in aid of the Society's funds. Harry has written with affection of his days at Worcester.

> At the special concert to commemorate what was then thought to be the centenary of the Society, Sir Adrian Boult was the guest conductor for a performance of Elgar's *Music Makers*. I remember having to play the piano for a rehearsal he took and finding it very difficult to follow his changes of speed from that enormous baton he used to wield, wound round with hundreds of rubber bands at the point where he held it!
>
> What I remember most about the Choral Society is the splendid people who sang in it. When I arrived, Wynne Tucker and Charles Flexman were Secretary and Treasurer and many people singing in the choir in 1963 went right back to the days of Elgar. Edgar Day himself had just retired in 1962 after a distinguished fifty years as assistant organist. He became a close friend – a wonderful source of anecdotes and information about Elgar, Atkins and many others in the musical scene going back to before the First World War.
>
> Don Parker is a person I remember very specially. He used to sit just next to my right ear at rehearsals, singing with his usual verve and vigour, which was sometimes an unnerving experience! In certain works, such as *The Dream of*

WORCESTER FESTIVAL CHORAL SOCIETY
and
CITY OF BIRMINGHAM SYMPHONY ORCHESTRA

VESPERS of 1610

MONTEVERDI

(edited by Walter Goehr)

Soloists:

DOREEN PRICE	ANGELA BEALE
CHARLES BRETT	WYNFORD EVANS
DAVID JOHNSTON	JOHN NOBLE

GLYN DAVENPORT

Choristers of Worcester Cathedral

Harpsichord: STEPHEN CLEOBURY

Organists: HARRY BRAMMA
ANDREW MILLINGTON

Viola da Gamba: TREVOR JONES

Cello Continuo: JOHN FRANCA

Double Bass Continuo: GEORGE GREER

CITY OF BIRMINGHAM SYMPHONY ORCHESTRA

(Leader: FELIX KOK)

Conductor: CHRISTOPHER ROBINSON

SATURDAY, 3rd NOVEMBER, 1973

WFCS programme extract (courtesy Marjorie Potts)

WORCESTER
FESTIVAL
CHORAL SOCIETY

The Hymn of Jesus
(Holst)

St. Paul's Suite
(Holst)

Four Sacred Pieces
(Verdi)

Saturday, 9th March, 1974, at 7.30 p.m.

WFCS programme (courtesy Marjorie Potts)

Gerontius, he claimed to know the score by heart and sat with his hands folded in front of him, his eyes never once leaving the conductor's baton! His particular party piece was the impressive tune for the tenors, 'He that walketh upon the wings of the wind' from *The Kingdom* by Elgar. Don claimed that he had been personally complimented by Elgar himself on a number of occasions for his performance of this particular passage. So one could go on.

As well as singing in regular performances each season and in the 'away' concerts already referred to, members were among the congregation for the 1968 'Songs of Praise' televised from the Cathedral; and in 1973 they sang in the cathedral with members of the City of Birmingham Choir (of which Christopher Robinson was, and still is, the chorus master) in a full-length *St Matthew Passion* given as a devotional act on Maundy Thursday. There were also two 'gift' concerts, for the Society's funds. In 1971, a delightful performance of Rossini's *Petite Messe Solennelle* was given in Perrins Hall: Stephen Darlington and Andrew Millington have already been mentioned as the pianists; Harry Bramma was at the organ, and among the soloists were two other friends of the Society – Catherine Robinson, alto (the conductor's sister) and Henry Sandon, bass. In 1974, Gerald English expressed his wish to give a song recital, the proceeds from which would be a farewell tribute to Christopher Robinson, who would accompany him. This enjoyable recital was also held in Perrins Hall.

The Society's finances were a source of some anxiety, only partially relieved by the concerts and recitals described above. There were modest, but enjoyable, efforts from individual members, often in their own homes, and in 1973 a Grand Auction sale 'conducted' by Ian Pattison raised nearly £700. The various attempts to hold purely social, as distinct from money-making, functions have, with a few notable exceptions, never been wholly successful, perhaps because choral singers and their professional masters are all very busy people who want to meet in order to sing, and also because many of the chorus have to travel into Worcester from some distance. There were two dinners, however, during this period, one at the Star Hotel in 1967 and one at the Giffard Hotel the following year, both of which were well attended and successful. The Cheese-and-Wine party at Hartlebury Castle on 1 May 1970, organized by Isobel Anderson and hosted by the Bishop, Dr Mervyn Charles Edwards, the Society's President, was a fine celebration of what has proved not to be the Society's centenary year. Sir Arthur Bliss, Sir Adrian Boult, Dr Douglas Guest, Heather Harper and the Very Rev and Mrs R L P Milburn were among those who sent congratulatory telegrams; there was also a message from Isobel Baillie; and a toast to the Society was proposed by John Carol Case. The birthday cake was cut by Edgar Day, who spoke of his sixty-one years' association with WFCS.

The Right Rev Eric Kemp, the present Bishop of Chichester, sang with the Society for some years when he was Dean of Worcester, as did his wife. Of those years he writes:

> My wife and I moved to Worcester, having both been members of the Oxford Bach Choir for a good many years in which we had derived great enjoyment and pleasure from singing so many of the fine great choral works. We therefore looked forward very much to being able to continue this experience in the Worcester Festival Chorus. Happily we were both accepted by Christopher Robinson, who had been an accompanist for the Oxford Bach Choir during part of the time that we sang there. We found that the Worcester Festival Chorus was of a somewhat different order from the Oxford Bach Choir which was an essentially amateur organisation founded by Sir Hugh Allen to give to as wide extent as possible of undergraduates and other Oxford people the experience of singing the great choral works. The Worcester Festival Chorus by its participation in the Three Choirs Festival was of a more nearly-professional character . . . [We] greatly enjoyed and valued our time in the Chorus and we learned a great deal from the training and conducting of Christopher Robinson, whom I still regard as one of the best choral conductors under whom I have sung. We also had the great privilege for one of the concerts of singing under the conductorship of Sir Adrian Boult, who managed to achieve fine results with what one might call minimalist conducting.

The 1974 *Messiah* on 3 December was Christopher Robinson's last concert before leaving Worcester to take up his new appointment as Organist and Master of the Choristers at the Chapel Royal, Windsor. After the performance, members, patrons and friends filled College Hall for a farewell party and presentation to Christopher and his wife. There followed Richard Holding's medley, 'This is your life', conducted by Robin Mack Smith and sung by a special Demi-Semi-Chorus. It is impossible to recapture the flavour of this in mere words without their music, but one recalls, perhaps, a verse which points with wit to Christopher's constant attention to precision of detail:

'Christopher, Christopher, where have you been?'
'I've been up to Windsor to visit the Queen.'
'Christopher, Christopher, what did you there?'
'I looked for the dotted notes under her chair.'

Christopher Robinson's fine musicianship, sensitive and exacting, his insistence on accuracy and on clarity of diction, combined with his personal humility, his warmth and sincerity, ensured that he gave much to WFCS. It is good that he, too, remembers his time as 'twelve happy years'.

Donald Hunt (courtesy Three Choirs Festival Committee)

10

DONALD HUNT (1975 - 1996)

When Donald Hunt came to Worcester in 1975 he was the first of the seven WFCS conductors since 1861 with experience as the regular conductor of other big choral societies. William Done and Ivor Atkins had learnt on the job over long years (as had Hugh Blair for a shorter time), whilst Donald Hunt's three immediate predecessors, though by no means without experience of choral society conducting, were taking on the responsibility for WFCS near the beginnings of their careers.

Donald Hunt was born in Gloucester, where he was a cathedral chorister under Herbert Sumsion, to whom he was then articled, becoming Gloucester's assistant organist at the age of seventeen. In 1954, he was appointed organist of St John's Church, Torquay, and three years later went as Director of Music to Leeds Parish Church, where he stayed for seventeen years. During those years he taught at the Leeds College of Music, founded the Yorkshire Sinfonia Orchestra in 1971, and, the following year, was appointed to a post which Leeds had allowed to lapse for fifty years – that of City Organist. Nurtured on Gloucestershire/West Country music with its Elgarian and pastoral associations, he soon came to know and understand a different musical tradition – that of the West Riding choral societies. He became conductor of the Halifax and the Leeds Philharmonic Societies and Associate Conductor and Chorus Master of the Leeds Festival.

In May 1975, Leeds University recognized his services to their city and county by awarding him an honorary doctorate. Five months earlier, he had succeeded Christopher Robinson at Worcester, and in August of that year he directed his first

Three Choirs Festival. Donald Hunt brought to WFCS, therefore, his experience of handling big North Country choirs, doubtless containing many forthright Yorkshire members proud of traditions which went back further than Worcester's. At the same time, since Herbert Sumsion and Edgar Day had both retired, as Sumsion's former pupil, Donald Hunt was, and is, the closest link in the Three Choirs with Elgar and his music, and quickly revealed his innate feeling for the Elgarian style. The Society was therefore delighted when Donald Hunt's great contribution to English music was recognised in 1993 by the award of an OBE.

Dr Hunt's programmes have presented a carefully-chosen blend of traditional and new, of long-time favourites and lesser-known, sometimes new, modern works, and among them his special interest in French music has found eloquent expression. The great baroque masses and oratorios have continued to inspire, even in an age when musical scholarship and taste favour their performance by much smaller choirs. Donald Hunt's *Messiah,* with its tonal qualities well graded from the light, dancing first and second parts to the mighty sonorities of Part III, has presented a successful compromise between the stylistic demands of Handel's original scoring and the performance by a choir of more than two hundred voices.

Of note among the annual performances have been 1976, when some of the soprano solos were memorably sung by a cathedral chorister, Jonathan Nott; and the conductor's hundredth performance in 1980, when the chorus included representatives from societies and choirs with which Donald Hunt is, or was, associated – the choral societies of Halifax and Scunthorpe, Leeds Philharmonic Society, and the Worcester Cathedral Choir. Bach and Mozart, the mighty *Missa Solemnis* of Beethoven, the excitement of Verdi's *Requiem* and of Mendelssohn's less frequently-heard *Elijah* have all been part of the Society's experience of the music of the past during the last two decades, as well as shorter works like the Requiems of Cherubini, Brahms and Dvořák, Rossini's *Stabat Mater* and Verdi's *Four Sacred Pieces.*

Now standing near the site of the Elgar music shop, and facing the Cathedral, is the statue of Sir Edward Elgar, unveiled by HRH the Prince of Wales after the Royal Elgar Concert in June 1981. Of the Society's many Elgar peformances it is difficult for anyone involved with them to write with detachment. Testimony to what Elgar

Donald Hunt rehearsing WFCS, 1978 (courtesy Roderick Attwood)

means to WFCS and to Worcester has come, however, from a member of the audience, Jeannine Alton, who writes as follows:

> Among the pleasures of a lifelong friendship with the author of this history has been the recurring opportunity to attend choral concerts in the cathedral.
>
> There have been so many of these happy and uplifting occasions: sometimes there was the chance to sit in on a rehearsal and enjoy the transmutation from jeans and sandals to the evening's formal gear; sometimes there was the privilege of joining the choir's forgatherings and supper in the august Old Palace; sometimes, in the summer, the ancient buildings lay open to the streaming sun; in the winter, they glowed a welcome. Always there was the presence or the anticipation of music, giving a rhythm and a spring to one's being.
>
> With such a store of memories, how to choose without unfairness? It can't be done. But there is one that catches so much of the essence of the choir, the cathedral, the years of dedication to music and worship, and epitomises all they mean to me and, I felt unmistakably, to everyone who shared it.
>
> It was February 1984. The 900th anniversay celebrations of the Cathedral. The 50th anniversary of the death of Elgar, if not the city's greatest son then surely the best-loved. The work? *The Dream of Gerontius,* of course, so often performed in this place, with these forces, but never so charged with feeling. The vast choir, disciplined and versatile in the multiple roles the composer lays upon it, combined with the Royal Liverpool Philharmonic Orchestra to steer us through that mysterious journey from mortal fear to sublimity.
>
> I'm not going to write about the specifically musical aspects of the evening. I was more aware of the – audience? congregation? participants rather. The sense of continuity, communal memory, shared experience was palpable. Everywhere around me people were recalling, reminding, pooling reminiscences. Many of them were from families who, somewhere along the line, actually remembered Elgar or had connections with him, or – of course – had themselves sung the work. Perhaps these really were his Dream Children. Behind me a couple were almost in tears because they hadn't managed to buy a programme. When I gave them mine, I knew it would instantly become an heirloom. Although I had sensed for years the symbiosis between that work and that place, the reality of the mesh that binds us to history and to one another became overpoweringly manifest that night. This would not have surprised Elgar. 'You must come to Worcester and hear what *Gerontius* might be,' he wrote. 'The building will do it.' He was right.

Singers throughout 'Three Choirs Country' have a special affection for twentieth-century English music with what may be termed 'Gloucestershire, Pastoral'

'You must come to Worcester and hear what *Gerontius* might be – the building will do it.' Edward Elgar.

WFCS in Worcester Cathedral, 1986 (courtesy Roderick Attwood)

associations: Vaughan Williams's *Sancta Civitas*, Holst's *Hymn of Jesus*, Finzi's *Intimations of Immortality*, all of which have been heard since 1975. Of the bigger twentieth-century choral works have been performances of Tippett's *A Child of Our Time* (1975), Britten's *War Requiem* and Walton's *Belshazzar's Feast* (1977 and 1984). That neither of the first two had been performed for nearly twenty years may reflect a turning away from works inspired by two world wars, or perhaps a change in the assessment of these works. Christopher Robinson used to maintain (and presumably still does) that, of the two, Tippett's was the greater and would outlast Britten's. Donald Hunt wrote at the time of the 1978 performance of the *War Requiem* that, despite Britten's genius, grave doubts had come to be expressed about the work's effect: 'Did it not help to perpetuate, or immortalize, the very concept that both poet and composer abhorred?' Whatever the musicians' judgement, there cannot be the same controversy concerning the emotive, one might almost say the religious, impact of the splendid clamour of Walton's *Belshazzar's Feast*.

Among more recent works the Society has sung Bernstein's *Chichester Psalms*, Fanshawe's *African Sanctus* (given its British première by the Society in the 1978 Festival), Matthias's *Let us now praise Famous Men* and Roxburgh's *The Rock*. The last named was a first performance, attended by the composer and recorded for broadcasting. Edwin Roxburgh has based his work on the 'Worcester Fragments', fourteenth-century manuscripts found early this century, some wrapped round bundles of accounts and some used for bookbinding, and providing the earliest evidence of music of the period. The performance was a successful and happy occasion and was followed by a Civic Reception in the Guildhall.

Donald Hunt has given three concerts of French music (1977, 1983 and 1994), and the first of these was attended by the French Cultural Attaché, M. Ives Mabin and his wife. The 1983 concert was particularly memorable for its performance of Villette's *Messe en Français* (first given at the 1981 Three Choirs Festival). The composer and his wife came, not only to the concert but to the final rehearsal in the Chapter House, and afterwards Mme Villette wrote to Dr and Mrs Hunt, '. . . so we are back in Aix ... and I want to tell you the pleasure we had, Pierre and I, when we were at Worcester. Everything was perfect: your warm hospitality, the choir and musicians, friendship with everyone . . . Thank you for everything and kind regards

To Donald Hunt

With warmest congratulations
and thanks for a magnificent
performance; it was far beyond
my wildest expectations.
Please extend my thanks and
appreciation to the Worcester Chorus
for such valiant and rewarding work.

Edwin Roxburgh

22 · III · 80 ·

Edwin Roxburgh 'The Rock': manuscript inscription to Donald Hunt following the first performance
(courtesy Edwin Roxburgh and Worcester Cathedral Library)

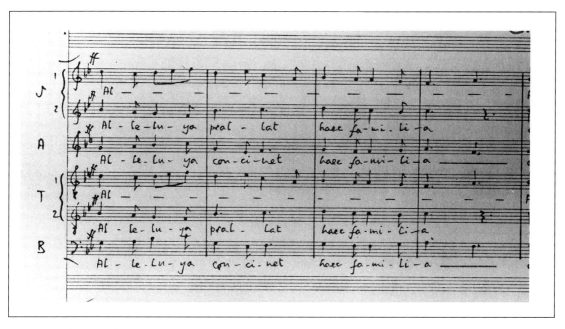

Edwin Roxburgh 'The Rock': extract from manuscript showing 'Worcester Fragments'
(courtesy Edwin Roxburgh and Worcester Cathedral Library)

to your friends who are now ours also. A lot of kisses from us both.' M. Villette added, 'Merci encore'. In the same concert, Fauré's *Requiem* had a special poignancy as it commemorated three musicians connected with Worcester and the Three Choirs, who had all died shortly before the concert: Sir Adrian Boult (one of the Society's Vice Presidents), Dr Herbert Howells and Edgar Day.

Throughout these years there were several special occasions in which WFCS participated. In 1980, the Worcester Diocese commemorated its thirteen hundredth anniversary, and in May, on the County cricket ground, at a celebration of the Eucharist by the Archbishop of Canterbury, members of the Society sang 'The Spirit of the Lord' from *The Apostles* and 'How lovely are thy dwellings fair' from Brahms's *Requiem.* The following month, during a special music week, a concert of Choral Praise included Haydn's *Te Deum*, Mozart's *Coronation Mass* and Handel's two Coronation Anthems, *The King shall rejoice* and *Zadok the Priest.* In 1986 the City of Birmingham Symphony Orchestra invited the Society to take part in a Spring Festival and to sing Britten's *Spring Symphony*. 'Extra-curricular' occasions for several years were 'Carols for All' in which WFCS participated.

The concert of 'Sounding Brass and Voices' in October 1989, when the John Foster Black Dyke Mills Band sounded its very accomplished brass and percussion and WFCS provided the voices for songs outside their usual repertoire, had an enthusiastic reception; and songs such as 'The Long Day Closes' and 'The Holy City' were surely a reminder of what the Society and its audiences heard many years earlier in the days of their Public Hall concerts.

In 1990 and 1991 the major repairs to the cathedral meant that WFCS had to find another concert hall, and after much deliberation Worcester's Perdiswell Leisure Centre was chosen. Though its situation on the outskirts of the city and the mere fact of its not being 'The Cathedral' made it unpopular with some of the regular members of the audience, its acoustic proved surprisingly better than anticipated; and it also enabled the Society to present secular music and so to learn different works that were new to them. Orff's *Carmina Burana*, a concert of sea music including Stanford's *Songs of the Fleet*, and a welcome return, after seventy years or so, of Coleridge-Taylor's *Hiawatha's Wedding Feast*, were much enjoyed by singers and audience, as was another 'Sounding Brass and Voices' Concert.

WFCS programme (courtesy Marjorie Potts)

WORCESTER FESTIVAL CHORAL SOCIETY

Saturday 19 November 1994, 7.00 p.m.

WORCESTER CATHEDRAL

Hector

BERLIOZ

Messe Solennelle

FRANCK - Psaume CL

FAURE - Pavane

BIZET - Te Deum

LONDON GALA ORCHESTRA

Melanie Armistead

Philip Dennis

Alan Fairs

DONALD HUNT : CONDUCTOR

WFCS programme (courtesy Marjorie Potts)

For both singers and audience the understanding and appreciation of many of the major, and the new, works have been enriched by the talks about them given by Dr Hunt shortly before their performance. Another innovation during the 1970s and 1980s has been the link with Halifax Choral Society, for which Donald Hunt and Simon Lindley shared responsibility and which, founded in 1815, can claim to be the oldest choral society in Britain. In November 1976, some members from Halifax joined the Society for the Verdi *Requiem,* and later that same month some of WFCS went to Halifax for a performance of Richard Rodney Bennett's *Spells.* Members from Halifax participated, too, in the Cathedral's 900th centenary festival concert already referred to.

As well as visiting Halifax, WFCS has sung in several cities throughout the country. In 1978, the Society performed Williamson's *Mass of Christ the King* in Westminster Cathedral, and two years later it was back in London, invited by the Elgar Foundation, to sing *The Apostles*, conducted by Donald Hunt, in the Royal Albert Hall. WFCS had previously sung for the Foundation at the same venue in 1978 presenting Elgar's *The Music Makers* in the presence of HRH the Prince of Wales who met members of the chorus at the reception afterwards. An invitation to the King's Lynn Festival came the following year, for performances of *Gerontius* (conductor Vernon Handley) and Fanshawe's *African Sanctus* (conductor Donald Hunt) on two successive nights. That visit is memorable for the warm hospitality given to members in various homes in King's Lynn, and for David Fanshawe's exuberant flinging of carnations among the audience at the end of the performance of his work. In 1984 came a visit to Liverpool's Anglican Cathedral when WFCS joined with the Liverpool Welsh Choral Union for *The Apostles*, conducted by Sir Alexander Gibson. The vast building with its difficult acoustic seemed to create such a distance between chorus and audience that the impact of the work was perhaps more telling for those who listened to the live broadcast. More recently have come visits by members of the Society to Birmingham Town Hall in 1988 for Christmas music directed by Adrian Partington, and visits to the Symphony Hall in 1991 and 1993, joining the BBC Singers and the BBC Symphony Chorus for performances of *Gerontius* and *The Kingdom* in aid of the Elgar Birthplace Appeal. Also in 1991 the Society went to Bridgnorth for a performance of *Messiah.*

With Honegger's *King David* in April 1992, performed on the centenary of the composer's birth, the Society returned to the Cathedral, but not to what had become its customary west end platform. The new platform in the crossing under the tower, the position from which Douglas Guest had succeeded in moving the chorus, means that much of the sound, however well projected, is swallowed in the heights of the tower. The glorious 'Et Resurrexit' in the fine 1995 performance of Bach's *B Minor Mass*, for instance, was thus denied its full triumphant power.

Among the performances since 1992 was a memorable one in March 1993 when the Society welcomed back its former conductor, Sir David Willcocks, always a good friend of WFCS. He conducted Vaughan Williams's *Five Mystical Songs*, and in the same programme his son, Jonathan – born in Worcester – conducted his own composition *Voices of Time*.

Malcolm Williamson's *Procession of Palms*, Stainer's *Crucifixion* (a first-time performance for WFCS), an *Elijah* in November 1993 for the first time for eleven years, a French concert the following year – these, together with *Gerontius,* the *B Minor Mass* and the Christmas *Messiahs,* have marked three good years since the return from Perdiswell. The mezzo-soprano soloist who sang in the *B Minor Mass* was Catherine King, a former member of the Society, who writes:

> I joined WFCS at the tender age of fourteen and was launched with a bang and a shock into rehearsals for *Belshazzar's Feast*. It was an exciting and noisy way to start, with a large choir and orchestra and a bird's eye view from the top row of the stands. I was relieved to get my 'slain' in the right place.
>
> It was an easy set-up for me to fit into. We could have taken out family membership with my father and older sister also singing, and even Andrew as a chorister joining in on occasions. There was a thriving youth section in the Choral Society, too, and older members were also friendly and welcoming.
>
> On the musical front it was a great training ground with some wonderful and high-class music-making. I managed to fit in four Three Choirs Festivals before leaving for university, and those weeks of concentrated singing, camping in the various cathedral grounds, hold special memories of fun and involvement.
>
> Coming back to sing for Donald and the WFCS as a soloist has been very special for me. It feels slightly odd to be out at the front after the years on the raisers – I don't get such a good view of Donald's winks and frowns – but it is a good feeling to have so much support from friends behind me – literally. I owe a lot to WFCS.

*Donald Hunt rehearsing WFCS in 'The Music Makers' in the Royal Albert Hall in 1978
(courtesy Roderick Attwood)*

*Reception following the 1978 Albert Hall performance. The trio in the centre of the picture are (from
left to right) Marjorie Potts, Donald Hunt and HRH Prince of Wales (courtesy Roderick Attwood)*

The work of the chorus and its conductor owes an immeasurable debt to the accompanists, as it has done since the foundation of the Society. In 1976 Harry Bramma, now Principal of the Royal School of Church Music, was appointed organist of Southwark Cathedral, and his place was taken by Paul Trepte, now organist at Ely Cathedral. Paul has written the following about his Worcester experience:

Three weeks ago today I had the thrill of conducting Verdi's *Requiem* in the splendid surroundings of Ely Cathedral. The choir, numbering about 280 singers, was an extremely amateur group known as the Cambridge Village Colleges Choral Society. It was founded by a former conductor of the Worcester Festival Choral Society, Sir David Willcocks. There is no audition for membership! The orchestra for our Verdi performance was a much expanded Hertfordshire Chamber Orchestra, comprising players with varying degrees of skill . . .

I was aware, as I launched into the final three hour rehearsal with this very mixed bunch of enthusiastic performers, that a truly intimate knowledge of the score on my own part was to be an essential and assured factor in achieving a successful performance. The confidence I experienced on this level was due entirely to knowledge gained at Worcester. There is no better way of getting to know a score than by accompanying the work at the piano keyboard - the traditional role of assistant organists at Worcester! Memories of rehearsing the Verdi under Donald Hunt come flooding back. My favourite one concerns a page turn in the 'Dies Irae'. All those cascading semiquavers are great fun to play, and there is a gift of an opportunity in this movement for any rehearsal pianist to release any amount of aggression by bashing the piano with relish! In my enthusiasm, I ripped out the whole page which went flying into the face of an unsuspecting soprano, much to the amusement of all assembled in the Chapter House. I always remember this whenever I come to the sellotaped page in my vocal score!

I shall take this opportunity to pay homage not only to Worcester Festival Choral Society, but also to my teacher and mentor, Donald Hunt. It was he who first gave me the opportunity to learn this part of my trade by appointing me, at the tender age of 14, accompanist to the Halifax Choral Society. I never looked back, and I am still as aware as ever that a good accompanist is as essential as a good conductor when working with large choral societies. It meant a great deal to me (as well as to Donald) when members of the Halifax Choral Society joined the Worcester Society on the occasion of a certain conductor's 100th *Messiah* performance. It also meant a great deal to me when I was given the opportunity to conduct part of a concert with Worcester Festival Choral Society.

I took charge for a performance of Mozart's Symphony No. 21 and the same composer's *Coronation Mass*. I got the speed of the first movement of the symphony wrong, and I vividly remember being caught out at the beginning of the Credo, because I thought we were about to sing the Sanctus! We all have to make these sorts of mistakes if we are to learn, but I remain eternally grateful for the good humoured patience of all those singers in Worcester who tolerated such errors of judgement.

The singing tradition at Worcester is one of the greatest of its type in the world. The succession of fine musicians who have been privileged to steer it and the devotion of those who turn up week by week to sing account for this truth. There are those who claim that music making of this sort is a dying art. If there is truth in this view we can be sure that Worcester will continue to perpetuate the fine tradition – not only because they love their Elgar – but also because they are always prepared to tackle something new.

Thank you, Worcester Festival Choral Society, for all you contributed to my own growth as a musician, and for all the pleasure you will continue to give to so many audiences.

In 1981 Paul, having married one of the Society's altos, went to be organist at St Mary's, Warwick. Adrian Partington, who took his place, was a former Worcester chorister, subsequently organ scholar at King's College, Cambridge, and described by Donald Hunt as 'a brilliant musician and gifted accompanist' – and so it proved. Adrian's observations, when asked for his impressions shortly after his return to Worcester, were of the Society's larger and more ambitious repertoire. He added, 'I have the impression that there are fewer tenors and basses than there used to be, but considerably more sopranos. Thus the top line is always extremely audible, both when singing and when talking during rehearsal.' In 1991, Adrian left to go as Director of Music at Abbot's Bromley School and his place was taken by Raymond Johnston, a former organ scholar of Peterhouse, Cambridge, who came to Worcester from a post as assistant director of music at Ellesmere College, Shropshire.

The other accompanist still so warmly remembered is Edgar Day. King's School boys of much later generations had kept in constant touch with him and visited him in his home. There, too, Wynne Tucker used to visit him, as she recalls, every Wednesday morning up to the time of his death; 'how he loved,' she says, 'to chat over old times.' After a lifetime of devoted service to the Cathedral and the Choral Society he died in 1983 at the age of 92. The many references to him from

Edgar Day (photograph Brendan Kerney, courtesy Donald Hunt)

contributors to this history testify to the high regard and respect he inspired in all generations throughout the greater part of this century. Wulstan Atkins remembers how, in 1914, he and his fellow probationers saved their pennies to buy him a birthday present 'because we loved him'. That Edgar Day lived in Edgar Street and composed an anthem 'Round me falls the night' (by Day) always aroused a smile, but it was a smile of the warmest affection for this humble, loyal, gentle man – a 'good and faithful servant', a gifted musician, a true gentleman.

Once a choral society is securely established, its history is concerned mainly with the music it makes and those who direct it, but for it to continue as a living organism there must be changes and developments. Rules must be revised from time to time, as a glance at the contents of the 1861 Rule Book (pages 19 - 20) makes clear. WFCS rules were revised in 1977, and whilst they mainly confirm the earlier provisions for the Society's administration, there are innovations. The Diocesan Bishop had originally, and for very many years, been President *ex officio*; from 1977 the AGM was to elect its President, though in fact up to the present time it always has elected the Bishop. Rule 11 makes clear that an audition on entry to the Society may be only the first of such tests over the years. The booklet opens with a grandiose statement of the Society's aims: 'To educate the public in the arts and sciences, and in particular the art and science of choral music, by the presentation of concerts and other activities . . .' Perhaps this was to satisfy the Charity Commissioners in order that WFCS could be registered with them. In 1988 came an important addition to these rules: the conductor and accompanist were to be engaged by the Committee by written contract. By a strange coincidence, this new Rule Book was drawn up exactly a hundred years after the reconstitution of the Society, in the days, long past, when 'gentlemen's agreements' were not considered to need formalizing in writing. Rising musical standards – despite all that is said and written about present-day falling standards in general – make the rule about auditions essential.

In the 1970s, concern was expressed at the decline in the number of young members of student age, and it was therefore encouraging that in the 1978 *St Matthew Passion* the ripieno part was once more provided by a school – this time the choir of Christopher Whitehead Girls' School. In 1991, a member of the chorus, having produced an audience survey report, stressed the need to attract more school students and people in the 20-30 age-group. Stemming from this came a schools concert in 1993, organized by City and County music teachers, in which about four hundred schoolchildren took part, the proceeds from which went to a special fund to provide tickets for schools for WFCS concerts.

Other initiatives by individual members have been the designing of the WFCS logo, and a newsletter, compiled and edited by Richard Holding and appearing two or three times a year from 1981 to 1987. There have, too, been social activities: parties for new members; farewell parties for assistant organists and for retiring officers, and one after the performance of Elgar's *The Light of Life* for Wulstan Atkins on the occasion of his eightieth birthday.

Inevitably there have been, as in any organization, disappointments, difficulties, problems. There was the performance of Malcolm Williamson's *Mass of Christ the King* on the composer's fiftieth birthday, when he did not make his expected appearance, and when the BBC, unknown to WFCS, broadcast the work on the same night. There have been, too, misunderstandings, though they have been few, and satisfactorily resolved. The greatest problem has been financial, at one time threatening the Society's continued existence. The economic straits of the country in the early 1990s were in part responsible for a situation also faced by many other choral societies. The weather made the second year at Perdiswell financially disastrous, as *Messiah* and 'Sounding Brass and Voices' had to be postponed because of blizzards; and although both concerts took place later, audiences were disappointingly small.

The need over the last two decades of the century to raise money revealed hidden gifts, other than musical ones, as members secured sponsorships for parachute jumps, for knitting, and for a host of enterprises in between. Weekly raffles and bring-and-buy sales, an auction sale, open gardens, a '100 Club' and many other activities not only helped the finances but drew people more closely together. Meanwhile, to raise the larger resources essential for every concert today, sponsorships from firms and businesses were widely sought.

As this history of the Society draws to its end, it is time to acknowledge the immense debt owed to committee members and especially to the Officers, all of whom, for well over a century, have given so much of their time, as well as their ability, with generosity, goodwill and humour. For fourteen years, from 1962 to 1976, Wynne Tucker's work as Secretary was exemplary, and when she and the Treasurer, Charles Flexman, retired, College Hall was filled for a party on the morning of 4 December 1976, when they were both presented with cheques. Wynne Tucker's work as secretary is, at the time of writing, being carried on by Marjorie Potts who continues to give dedicated and tireless service. Her encyclopaedic knowledge of Society members (and their families) and her caring attitude have over the years been greatly appreciated by members of WFCS. The Chairman of the Society was traditionally either the Dean or a member of the Chapter, until 1987, when the Very Rev Tom Baker retired from the office. Since then, the Chairman has been an elected member of the chorus. To all those who have steered the Society through times both difficult and happy, much is owed.

WFCS gave its first concert in 1861 in a city with a population of only about 32,000. By the time Ivor Atkins came, at the turn of the century, there were half as many again – about 46,600 – and by the time of his retirement about 70,000. During the last forty years that figure has risen by another 10,000. As the city more than doubled in size, so did WFCS, though the revolution in travel has meant that a far higher proportion now come from the county. The chorus numbers at the time of writing, about 220, a little lower than those of a few years ago, would seem to be a good representation for the city and county.

As the population has grown, the old Worcester, so often nostalgically recalled, has been transformed. Memories of the Society's long association with the Public Hall and its occasional use of the Theatre Royal, can be visually revived only by old photographs; and the need for a full-sized concert hall worthy of the city has still not been met. As WFCS moves through its second century, there can be a reasonable assumption, however, that the Cathedral and its Chapter House will be standing at least in 2061. May they continue to inspire the singing of *Gerontius* by faithful members of Worcester Festival Choral Society.

Donald Hunt (courtesy Roderick Attwood)

EPILOGUE

by Donald Hunt

Worcester Festival Choral Society is justly proud of its history. It makes good reading, and it also amply demonstrates the significant role that the Society has played in the development of choral music in the city and district, as well as its maintenance of an enviable standard of cultural activity to the benefit of its members and the community at large.

A colourful history and pride in achievements are all very well, but the real test of a choir's durability is in its approach to music-making in a contemporary situation, where the challenges are much greater than those faced by our forebears. At a time when many societies are falling by the wayside for lack of membership, audiences, or funding – or perhaps a lethal combination of all three – and others faced with continual repetition of undemanding 'consumer friendly' programmes in order to survive, WFCS would appear to be flourishing. Certainly a membership of around two hundred singers is being maintained, and no one can dispute the fact that the programmes have been wide-ranging and, on occasions, adventurous. The avant garde may have been neglected, but there are reasons for this : few composers have real regard for the choral tradition as we understand it, and the financial risks of going down this particular path are considerable. Audiences are no more fickle than they ever were, but they do have an innate suspicion of anything 'modern', invariably indicating their anxiety with their feet! This is to be regretted, for, if our choral culture is to make progress, audiences and singers must from time to time indulge in exploration.

Concerts of choral music are among the most expensive forms of music making, creating a constant financial challenge, if not worry. Apart from the normal rehearsal and running expenses, concerts involve the engagement of first-class soloists and orchestras, as well as the venue and publicity costs, and all the other hidden expenditure that contributes to the smooth operation of a leading choral society, and we would like to think that we are in that latter category. It should be remembered that, in addition to presenting leading singers to the local community, the Society is currently the only artistic group to be bringing major symphony orchestras to Worcester. In the past twenty years this enterprise has brought no fewer than ten national orchestras to the city, with the BBC Philharmonic Orchestra, the City of Birmingham Symphony Orchestra and the Royal Liverpool Philharmonic Orchestra being the most regular visitors, as well as several of the more regional professional groups. This represents a vast expenditure and vast courage by our Treasurer and his team, a task made all the harder by the disgraceful withdrawal of meaningful public funding to part of a national heritage. However, generous local sponsorship and substantial recognition of our work by the Foundation for Sport and the Arts has given us encouragement to plan for the future with guarded confidence.

Of course it is possible to cut costs by reducing the size of the orchestra or even dispensing with it, and using the much maligned organ as accompaniment; but this rarely gives satisfaction to either performer or listener. We should bear in mind that our audiences these days are much better informed and know only too well when they are being short-changed. The days have changed when 'patrons' would buy a season ticket and come uncomplaining to anything that was offered; selective concert-going is now the 'name of the game'. We are reminded often enough that, for the price of a hard seat at a concert, our potential audience can purchase a compact disc to hear in the comfort of their own home a performance which is near perfect, albeit created artificially. We know that a live performance creates a better atmosphere and frequently has a special sort of magic, but we have to be sure that the public understands these facts. That is part of the nature of our challenge – we must always strive for the highest standards and be aware of the music's stylistic requirements.

Donald Hunt rehearsing WFCS in the Chapter House, 1996
(these and the two photographs overleaf, courtesy Roderick Attwood)

Thinking of style takes our thoughts to repertoire. Contemporary views on musical scholarship suggest that the large chorus, a by-product of the Victorian age, is inappropriate for anything up to and including Beethoven, and the 'historically correct' movement is now even encroaching upon the nineteenth century. We shall soon have little left that is considered to be genuinely suitable for our type of choral activity. Yet it is possible to achieve a compromise as exhibited in our annual performance of *Messiah*, and should we be really denying the choral singer the opportunity of experiencing practical involvement in such masterpieces as Bach's *Mass in b* and *St Matthew Passion*, or works by Haydn and Mozart, to mention but a few areas under the threat of authenticity? However, with the music of Edward Elgar we are on safe ground, and one of the great strength of the Society's activities is its devotion to, and quality performances of, the works of the Worcester composer. Here we can provide historical, emotional and musical correctness without fear of contradiction, and is it not right that our Society should be seen as a champion for our own composer's work? If Worcester fails to be a 'Mecca' for fine, authentic performances of Elgar's music it would indeed be tragic, if not criminal. We should aim to make Worcester the equivalent of Salzburg or Bayreuth, and in this image the WFCS should always have a prominent role. After all, Elgar himself said, 'You must come to Worcester Cathedral to hear my music.'

Of course the Cathedral is a perfect setting for much more than Elgar's music, but medieval buildings also present problems of balance, acoustic, lines of vision, temperature and other disadvantages, which can be a hindrance to participants and audiences alike. There must be a future for wider experiences, including repertoire which is totally unsuitable for a place of worship, in a more relaxed surrounding. The Society will need to explore a wider field of activity if it is to have a significant role into the next century. We represent a major leisure activity, both as receivers and givers, and we owe it to everyone to be progressive. We cannot live just on our past, or adopt only a narrow vision.

In this fiercely competitive and commercial world it is necessary for ambitious choirs to be engaged in media activity, and in this respect the Society has made great strides forward. There has been involvement in six commercial recordings, some in conjunction with the Cathedral Choir and others in a 'solo' capacity; but it is in the field of broadcasting that the Society has achieved its greatest successes. No fewer than twelve broadcasts have been undertaken since 1978 and all with a BBC orchestra. In addition there have been studio broadcasts and invitations to join with other societies for broadcasts from Birmingham, Liverpool and London. The occasional television appearance should also be noted. All this is a valuable way of bringing the Society's work to a wider audience, as well as enhancing its prestige; it is also rewarding to the members and their supporters to realise that they are among the elite group of amateur choruses who are eligible to work with a BBC orchestra – a privilege not accorded to many.

Members have also distinguished themselves by taking part in 'extramural' activities such as the Cantores Sabriniensis chamber choir which, under the conductorship of Majorie Potts, carried off the first prize in the Ladies Choral section of the first Elgar Choral Festival. Perhaps this sort of activity is another way of expanding the work of the Society, and reaching a wider section of the community. The twinning of Worcester with Kleve in Germany and Le Vesinet in France should offer further opportunities of cultural exchange; we may have a longer tradition of choral singing than our European counterparts, but there is much that we can all gain by sharing our cultures. These are all avenues of creativity which should be explored.

One of the great advantages of a large choir is that the sound it makes is invariably better than that of its constituent parts! A shaky technique, a weak voice, an inability to grasp complex rhythmic patterns or indeed to read quickly, will go almost unnoticed amidst such large forces, and there is usually an assemblage of professional musicians around to lean on when necessary. Certainly, techniques demanded these days are greater than they used to be; there may not be so many singers in choral groups with soloistic skills (some teachers take the ill-informed view that it is harmful to those with soloistic aspirations), but overall, choralists have to be more discerning musicians. Big is not necessarily beautiful, but a large choir singing *pianissimo* – and in tune – is a wondrous sound, which Mahler certainly appreciated when he wrote his choral endings to the 2nd and 8th Symphonies. Nor can the thrill of a choral unison in the music of Elgar or Vaughan Williams fail to stir the heart when delivered by a full-throated large choir. These are musical experiences to treasure, and can only by achieved effectively by a skilled group such as that we are honouring in this book.

There is also little doubt that the Society benefits musically from the association of its members with the Three Choirs Festival: the extensive repertoire, the special disciplines of a smaller group for regional rehearsals, and unique involvement with the Festival itself, will inevitably bring rich rewards back to the benefit of the 'winter season'. It is interesting to note that until the turn of the century the local singers were not considered good enough to form the entire Festival Chorus – the members being drawn from the Cathedral Choirs, local societies and supplemented by large contingents from assorted choruses around the country. (Sadly, it has to be admitted, that Worcester was the last of the three venues to stop this iniquitous practice.) Although there is a selection process for membership of the chorus, and admission is not exclusively to the WFCS, it remains a valuable association.

All these things mentioned are contributory to the success of the choir, nor should we forget the invaluable contribution regularly made by the lay clerks of the Cathedral Choir, but there is more: all these individual skills and experiences must be combined with deep commitment and an essential team spirit. The combination of all of these elements, properly nurtured, creates the miracle that is choral singing. Sir Thomas Beecham is reputed to have said that 'the English may not like music, but they absolutely adore the noise it makes', and George Bernard Shaw wrote that 'hell is full of musical amateurs'. Yet the 'noise' made by 'amateur' singers is the very essence of a great national heritage, of which Worcester Festival Choral Society is an integral part.

The Society richly deserves its success. Let us face the future, confident that we can continue the great legacy handed to us by those early enthusiasts, and the long line of devoted servants of the choir – the same enthusiasm and devotion that are engendered by the present officers of the Society. For my part, I have been privileged to be a small part of its history, and touched to have been the recipient of such generosity, friendship and musical satisfaction from the members: the 'joy of singing' is indeed a reality here.

Bravo, Worcester Festival Choral Society! March on into the next century with pride, confidence, ambition and humility.

> O may we soon again renew that song,
> And keep in tune with heaven, till God ere long
> To his celestial consort us unite,
> To live with him, and sing in endless morn of light!

Milton, *Ode on a Solemn Music*

APPENDIX

WORCESTER FESTIVAL CHORAL SOCIETY PERFORMANCES

1862 - 1995

This Appendix, compiled from extant programmes and the Society's Minute Book, is a largely complete annual record of the Society's performances to the end of 1995. Any gaps or uncertainties are indicated in the text.

1862	12 June	Haydn: *The Creation*, parts 1 and 2
	4 November	Part I. Handel: *Acis and Galatea* (selections)
		Part II. A miscellany of songs
1863	January (no date)	Handel: *Messiah*
	16 April	Haydn: 'Spring' (from *The Seasons*)
1864	12 January	Part I. National Anthem, followed by part-songs by soloists
		Part II. Macfarren: *Christmas Cantata*
	15 March	Part I. Haydn: *Creation* (selections), Mendelssohn: *St Paul*
		Part II. Miscellany of songs
	21 June	Part I. Rossini: 'Fair as a Bride' (from *William Tell*)
		Part II. Benedict: *Richard Coeur de Lion*
1865	5 January	Handel: *Messiah* (selections)
	4 April	Handel: *Judas Maccabeus*
	3 June	Part I. Handel: *Acis and Galatea* (selections)
		Part II. Solo songs, solo cello, and selections from Rossini: *William Tell*
1866	9 May	Handel: *Samson* (selections)
	22 June	Part I. Handel: *Dettingen Te Deum*
		Part II. Haydn: *Creation* (selections)
	19 December	Part I. Hatton: *Robin Hood*
		Part II. Solo songs, followed by Schumann: *Gypsy Life*
1867	4 January	Handel: *Messiah*
	25 April	Part I. Romberg: *The Lay of the Bell*
		Part II. Miscellany of songs
	13 June	Handel: *Alexander's Feast*
	13 December	Part I. Locke: *Macbeth*, followed by song miscellany
		Part II. Macfarren: *Christmas Cantata*
1868	2 January	Handel: *Messiah*
	28 February	Mendelssohn: *St Paul*
		nb: Programme Note: 'The Organ recently erected in the Music Hall will be used for the first time on this occasion.'
	8 May	Part I. Bennett: *The May Queen*
		Part II. Miscellany of songs followed by Schumann: *Gypsy Life*
	28 December	Handel: *Messiah* (extra concert not included in subscription series)
1889	28 January	Blair: *An Ode* 'as a tribute to the memory of the late A R Quarterman'; Handel: *Judas Maccabeus*

1889	30 April	Cowen: *The Sleeping Beauty*; Mendelssohn: *Lorelei*; Handel: *Organ Concerto in B Flat*
	10 December	Brahms: *A Song of Destiny*; Beethoven: *Symphony in C*; Mendelssohn: *Athalie*
1890	18 February	Part I. F H Cowen: *St John's Eve* Part II. Handel: *Organ Concerto No 1, G Minor*; Handel: Various arias
	24 November	Stanford: *The Battle of the Baltic*; Gade: *Symphony in C Minor*; Gounod: *Selections from Faust*; Mackenzie: *March and chorus from The Bride*
1891	26 April	Handel: *Israel in Egypt*
1892	22 November	Sullivan: *The Golden Legend*; Wagner: Overture *Die Meistersinger von Nürnberg*
1893	18 April	Part I. Auber: *March;* Gibbons: *The Silver Swan*; Mendelssohn: *Capriccio in B Minor* (piano and orchestra); Elgar: *The Black Knight* (first performance) Part II. Works by Lassus, Cowen and Schumann (including *Gypsy Life*)
1894	17 January	Grand Gounod Memorial Concert: *The Redemption*
1895	no date	Mendelssohn: *The First Walpurgis Night;* Sullivan *In Memoriam*; Elgar: *Spanish Serenade* followed by madrigals and orchestral selections
1896	21 January	Beethoven: *Elegy* (in memory of the late Dr Done); Dvořák: *Spectre's Bride*
1897	no date	Part I. *National Anthem* (arr. Blair) Elgar: *Imperial March* followed by song miscellany Part II. Elgar: *Scenes from King Olaf*
1898	25 January	Part I. Goring Thomas: *Cantata The Swan and the Skylark* Part II. Haydn *Symphony No 12* - B Flat; Various part-songs
	26 April	Berlioz: *Faust*
1899	24 January	Part I. Stanford: *The Revenge*; Wagner: Song from *Tannhäuser*, (solo), Parry: '*Blest Pair of Sirens*' Part II. Sullivan: *Merchant of Venice* (masque), Sullivan: Cantata: *On Shore and Sea*
	19 April	Wagner: *The Flying Dutchman*
1900	18 January	Mendelssohn: *St Paul*
	3 May	Coleridge-Taylor: *Hiawatha's Wedding Feast* and *The Death of Minnehaha* (conducted by the composer), Tchaikovsky: Duet and Fantasy-Overture from *Romeo and Juliet*
1901	14 January	Miscellany Saint-Saens: *Prelude Le Deluge*; Tchaikovsky: *Valse from Serenade* Op. 48 No2; Elgar: *Serenade for strings*; C Lee Williams: *Choral song - Music*; various solo and part songs; Sullivan: *Song for men's voices: The long day closes* (conductors: Edward Elgar, C Lee Williams, Ivor Atkins
	23 April	Dvořák: *The Spectre's Bride*
	25 November	Miscellany, including two works composed and conducted by Horatio Parker: *Come Away* (composed for and dedicated to the Worcester Festival Choral Society) and 'Iam Sol Recedit Igneus' (from *St Christopher*); also Benjamin Godard: *Second Pianoforte Trio* – I Atkins, J W Austin, Jos Owen.
1902	6 February	Part I. Walford Davies: *The Three Jovial Huntsmen* (conducted by the composer); Coleridge-Taylor: *The Death of Minnehaha* and *Hiawatha's Departure*
	25 November	Handel: I*srael in Egypt*

1903	24 February	Part I. Strauss: *Wanderers Sturmlied*; Elgar: *Coronation Ode* (Conducted by the Composer);
		Part II. Tchaikovsky: *Overture - Romeo and Juliet*; Cornelius: *Vätergruft*; Wagner: Prize Song and Finale: *Die Meistersinger*
	17 November	Part I. Wagner: *Kaiser Marsch*; Bach: *Now hath salvation and strength* (8-part motet); Coleridge-Taylor: *Meg Blane;* Handel: song from *Acis and Galatea*.
		Part II. Elgar: *Sursum Corda* (for orchestra); MacCunn: *The Cameronian's Dream*; Dvorák: *Adagio & Allegretto* from Symphony in G; Mozart: Aria *Non piu andrai*
1904	16 February	Part I. Elgar: *King Olaf*.
		Part II. Wagner: *Tannhäuser* (Act III)
	9 November	Elgar: *Caractacus* (conducted by the composer)
1905	21 February	Part I. Lee Williams: *A Festival Hymn* (conducted by the composer) Popper: *Hungarian Rhapsody* (cello solo); Cornelius: *Liebe, dir ergeb' ich mich* (motet for 8 voices).
		Part II. Brahms: *Alto Rhapsody;* Brahms: *Liebeslieder Walzer*
	6 December	Part I. Walford Davies: *Everyman*.
		Part II. Hugh Blair: *Trafalgar* (conducted by the composer)
1906	19 April	Part I. Parry: *The Pied Piper of Hamelin* solo; Part songs, including two by I Atkins and one by Elgar.
		Part II. Beethoven: *Symphony in C Minor* (No 5): Grieg: *Recognition of Land*
	28 November	Part I. Atkins: *Hymn of Faith*.
		Part II. Wagner: *Lohengrin* - Act III
1907	4 April	Part I. Brewer: *A Song of Eden*; Humperdinck: *The Pilgrimage to Kevlaar;* Schubert: *Symphony No 8*.
		Part II. Brahms: *Alto Rhapsody*; Elgar: *From the Bavarian Highlands*.
	27 November	Part I. Sullivan: *Overture: In Memoriam*; Grieg: *At the Cloister Gate*, *Recognition of Land* and solo songs; Grieg: *Peer Gynt Suite No 1 Part II*.
		Part II. Grieg: *Song of Harold Harfager*; Tchaikovsky: 1*812 Overture*; Elgar: *The Snow*; songs by Schubert, Brahms and Lee Williams.
1908	19 February	Part I. Stanford: *Last Post*; Brahms: *A Song of Destiny*; songs arranged by Stanford and Somervell; Stanford: *Irish Rhapsody*.
		Part II. Stanford: *Phaudrig Crohoore*, and *Songs of the Sea* - conductor: Charles Villiers Stanford.
	24 November	Parts I & II. Bruch: *The Lay of the Bell*.
1909	23 February	Part I. Mackenzie: *The Dream of Jubal*. Part II. Elgar: *Symphony in A Flat*.
	17 November	Part I. Gounod: *Faust*.
		Part II. Elgar: *Go, song of mine* (chorus unaccompanied in 6 parts); Mozart: *Symphony in C Major*.
1910	19 April	Part I. Beethoven: *Symphony No 9*
		Part II. Miscellany: songs; and part-songs for chorus by Brahms and Elgar.
	29 November	Part I. Brahms: *Requiem*;
		Part II. Holloway: *Orchestral Suite*; solo songs.
1911	14 February	Part I. Walford Davies: *Solemn Melody* for organ and strings; Brahms: *Liebeslieder Walzer;* Handel: *Organ Concerto in F Major*; solo songs.
	5 December	Sullivan: *The Golden Legend*.
1912	26 February	Part I. Elgar: *King Olaf*;
		Part II. Brent-Smith: *Piano Concerto*.
	26 November	Part I. Elgar: *The Music Makers*; Wagner: Vorspiel & Liebestod from *Tristan*
		Part II. Coleridge-Taylor: *Hiawatha's Wedding Feast*; solo songs.

1913	1 April	Part I. Parry: *Blest Pair of Sirens*; Elgar: *Serenade for Strings* (conducted by the composer); Elgar: *Evening Scene* (part song): Scharwenka: *Andante Religioso*; solo songs. Part II. Brahms: *Part Songs*; Mozart: *Divertimento*; Wesley: *In Exitu Israel*; solo songs.
	25 November	Part I. Handel: *Concerto Grosso*; Brahms: *Three Eight-Part Motets*; solo songs. Part II. Gluck: *Orpheus: Act II*; Grainger: *Mock Morris*; solo songs.
1914	24 February	Part I. Vaughan Williams: *Toward the Unknown Region*; Dvořák: *Symphony No 5 in E Minor (New World)*. Part II. Debussy: *The Blessed Damozel*; Humperdinck: *The Pilgrimage to Kevlaar.*
	21 December	Handel: *Messiah.*
1919	16 December	Handel: *Messiah.*
1920	17 February	Coleridge-Taylor: *Hiawatha's Wedding Feast* and *Death of Minnehaha*; solo songs.
	30 November	Part I. Handel: *Acis and Galatea*; Part II. Palmgren: *Finnish Lullaby*; Mozart: *Serenade for Strings*; solo songs.
1921	19 April	Elgar: *Caractacus.*
	6 December	Part I. Bach: Motet for Eight Voices: *Be not afraid*; Bach: *Concerto for Strings and pianoforte*; solo songs. Part II: Elgar: *Serenade for Strings* and part songs 'My Love Dwelt in a Northern Land' and 'Death on the Hills'; Purcell: *Suite for Strings*, solo songs
1922	4 April	Bach: *Mass in B Minor.*
	12 December	Part I. Elgar: *King Olaf.* Part II. Wagner: *Overture: The Mastersingers.*
	28 December	Handel: *Messiah.*
1923	13 March	Part I. Holst: *Two Psalms*; Doret: *French Songs*; Weelkes: six-part motet: *Hosanna to the Son of David*; Bach: *Violin Concerto (E Major)*; Wesley: *In Exitu Israel*. Part II. Handel: *Organ Concerto (G Minor)* Parry: *Never Weather-beaten Sail* and *There is an old belief*; songs by Farrar, Boughton and Bridge.
	11 December	Part I. Holst: *Turn back, O Man;* Elgar: 6-part chorus *Go, song of mine*; Walford Davies: *Solemn Melody*; solo songs - Verdi and Weber. Part II. Elgar: Part-songs -*Fly, singing bird, fly,The Snow, Death on the Hills*; Handel: *Organ Concerto in B Flat*, Parry: *Jerusalem.*
1924	18 March	Part I. Mackenzie: *The Bride;* Mozart: *Sonata for Organ and Strings*; songs. Part II. Elgar: Part-songs: *Fly, singing bird, fly* and *The snow*; Parry: Peace (from *Cantata War and Peace*) and *Jerusalem*; solo songs.
	9 December	Part I. Dale: *Cantata Before the paling of the stars*; Bach: *Violin Concerto*; Purcell (arranged Reed) *Three pieces* for solo violin and string orchestra. Part II. Brent-Smith: *Concerto for 2 violins and strings;* Parry: *Never weather-beaten sail* and *There rolls the deep*; Holst: *Two Psalms*; solo songs.
1925	24 March	Part I. Holst: *Ode to Death*; Brahms: *Alto Rhapsody*; songs by Gluck, Handel, Atkins. Part II. Gluck: *Orpheus*, Act II; songs by Fauré and Debussy; solo songs.
	8 December	Mendelssohn: *Elijah.*
1926	16 March	Part I. Handel: *Israel in Egypt*. Part II. Holst: *Turn back, O man*; solo songs.
	30 November	Part I. Bach: *Christmas Oratorio.* Part II. Corelli: *Christmas Concerto*; Handel: *Concerto Grosso in B Minor*, solo songs.

1927	22 March	Part I. Bizet: *Carmen* (abridged concert edition).
		Part II. Solo songs.
	6 December	Part I. Bach: *Come, Jesu, Come*; Elgar: *Serenade for Strings*; Reed: *Elegy for String Orchestra and Organ.*
		Part II. Handel: *Masque Suite*; Brahms: *Liebeslieder Walzer;* Boughton: *Three Folk Dances*; solo songs.
1928	13 March	Elgar: *The Dream of Gerontius.*
	11 December	Part I. Brahms: *Four trios* for female voices.
		Part II. Wagner: *Tannhäuser.*
1929	12 February	Part I. Schubert: *Great is Jehovah*; Scarlatti: *Suite for strings*; Brent-Smith: *Choral Dances*; solo songs.
		Part II. Folk songs arranged by Vaughan Williams and Holst; Purcell: *Suite for strings*; solo songs.
	3 December	Part I. Coleridge-Taylor: *Tale of Old Japan.*
		Part II. Miscellaneous (main part of programme is missing).
1930	10 April	Elgar: *The Apostles.*
	2 December	Part I. Boyce: *Symphony No 8* (for strings); Constant Lambert: *The Rio Grande*; solo songs.
		Part II. Bach: *Concerto in D Minor* for Clavier and Strings; Elgar: Part songs for female voices *Fly, singing bird, fly* and *The Snow*; Elgar: *Serenade for Strings*; Holst: *Two Psalms*; solo songs.

For the period from 1931 to 1946, no programmes have been discovered. The list of works performed during these years has therefore been compiled from references in the Society's Minute Book.

1931	3 March	Elgar: *The Dream of Gerontius*
	1 December	Purcell: *King Arthur*
1932	23 February	Mendelssohn: *Walpurgisnacht*
	16 March	Brahms: *Requiem*
1933	27 November	Elgar: *King Olaf*
1934	no date	Miscellaneous programme.
1935	17 December	Part I. Walford Davies: *Everyman.*
		Part II. Mozart: *Symphony No 40;* songs by Vaughan Williams and Delius.
1936	1 December	MacCunn: *The Lay of the Last Minstrel;* Schubert: *Symphony No 8*
1937	2 March	Stanford: *Songs of the Fleet;* Brahms: *Alto Rhapsody.*
	30 November	Handel: *Messiah*
1938	1 March	Bizet: *Carmen.*
	29 November	German: *Merrie England*
1939	21 February	Purcell: *King Arthur;* Handel: *Concerto Grosso* for Strings; songs and part songs.
1946	16 March	Elgar: *The Kingdom*
	30 March	Brahms: *Requiem*
	27 November	Elgar: *The Music Makers;* Vaughan Williams: *Fantasia on Christmas Carols*; Schubert: *Symphony No 8 in B Minor*

1947	26 March	Elgar: *The Apostles*
	29 November	Holst: *Two Psalms*; Elgar: *Sursum Corda*; Atkins: Motet - *Behold I come quickly*; Beethoven: *Symphony No 4* (B Flat); Dvořák: *Te Deum*.
1948	6 March	Bach: *St Matthew Passion*
	7 December	Handel: *Messiah*
1949	30 March	Verdi: *Requiem*
	23 November	Bach: *Christmas Oratorio*; Vaughan Williams: *Fantasia on Christmas Carols*.
1950	21 March	Haydn: *The Creation*
	29 November	Bach: *Mass in B Minor*
1951	15 March	Julius Harrison: *Mass in C*; Schubert: *Symphony No 8 in B Minor*
	6 December	Handel: *Messiah*
1952	8 April	Bach: *St John Passion*
	14 November	Elgar: *The Dream of Gerontius*
	5 December	Handel: *Messiah*
1953	10 March	Holst: *Hymn of Jesus*; Brahms: *Variations on a theme by Haydn*; Vaughan Williams: *Flos Campi*; Fauré: *Requiem*
	5 June	Recital of choral and orchestral music in honour of the Coronation of Her Majesty Queen Elizabeth II: Hayes: *Fanfare 'Britannic'* (Band of the Worcestershire Regiment) *The National Anthem* (arranged Elgar); Parry: 'I was glad' Boyce: *Symphony No 8 in D Minor;* Handel: 'Zadok the Priest':Purcell: *Suite for String Orchestra;* Byrd: Motet 'O. Lord make thy servant, Elizabeth' sung by the Cathedral choir; Elgar: *Serenade for Strings*; Holst: *Psalm 148;* Vaughan Williams: *Fantasia on 'Greensleeves'*; Handel: 'The King shall rejoice';Parry: *Jerusalem*.
	6 November	Elgar: *The Apostles*
1954	27 January	Handel: *Messiah*
	13 February	Palestrina: *O bone Jesu, exaudi me;* Anthony Lewis: *A Tribute of Praise;* Parry: *Never weather-beaten sail;* and songs sung by Isobel Baillie.
	18 March	Bach: *St Matthew Passion*
	11 November	Purcell: *Suite in G Minor* for string orchestra; Parry: *Blest Pair of Sirens*; Mozart: *Eine Kleine Nachtmusik*; Mozart: *Requiem Mass*
	1 December	Handel: *Messiah*
1955	10 February	Samuel Wesley: *In Exitu Israel;* Zoltan Kodaly: *Jesus and the traders;* Charles Wood: *Glory and Honour and Laud*; and songs sung by William Herbert.
	16 March	Bach: *Mass in B Minor*.
	10 November	Mozart: *Exultate, Jubilate*; Mozart: *Mass in C Minor*.
	7 December	Handel: *Messiah*
1956	18 February	Byrd: *Sing joyfully* and *Justorum Animae*; Pergolesi: *Stabat Mater* (Cathedral choristers and contralto solo); Bach: *Come, Jesus, Come*; and songs sung by Norma Procter.
	21 March	Bach: *St Matthew Passion*
	7 November	Mendelssohn: *Elijah*
	5 December	Handel: *Messiah*
1957	27 March	Elgar: *The Dream of Gerontius*
	2 June	Elgar: *Centenary Service*
	6 November	Haydn: *St Cecilia Mass*; Bach: Four pieces from *D Major Suite*
	4 December	Handel: *Messiah*

1958	19 March	Verdi: *Requiem*
	29 October	Mendelssohn: *Elijah*
	9 December	Handel: *Messiah*

1959	6 May	Mozart: *Symphony No 35* in D (Haffner); Beethoven: *Mass in D*
	3 November	Brahms: *St Antoni Variations* for Orchestra; Brahms: *Requiem*
	15 December	Handel: *Messiah*

1960	23 March	Bach: *St John Passion*
	8 November	Haydn: *The Creation*
	7 December	Handel: *Messiah*

1961	22 March	Bach: *Mass in B Minor*
	14 November	Bach: *Christmas Oratorio*
	5 December	Handel: *Messiah*

1962	21 March	Elgar: *The Dream of Gerontius*
	30 October	Mozart: *Overture to the Magic Flute*; Beethoven: *Violin Concerto*; Fauré: *Requiem*
	4 December:	Handel: *Messiah*

1963	4 March	Berlioz: *The Childhood of Christ*
	12 November	Haydn: *The Nelson Mass*; Vaughan Williams: *Five Mystical Songs*
	10 December	Handel: *Messiah*

1964	3 March	Elgar: *The Kingdom*
	17 November	Handel: *Zadok the Priest*; Elgar: *Cello Concerto*; Mozart: *Requiem*
	15 December	Handel: *Messiah*

1965	23 March	Bach: *St Matthew Passion*
	2 November	Elgar: *The Dream of Gerontius*
	14 December	Handel: *Messiah* (Part I); Britten: *St Nicholas*

1966	1 March	Bach: *Mass in B Minor*
	15 November	Britten: *Variations on a Theme by Purcell*; Mozart: *Clarinet Concerto*; Walton: *Belshazzar's Feast*
	13 December	Bach: *Christmas Oratorio* (Parts I & II); Handel: *Messiah* (Selections)

1967	14 March	Bruckner: *Mass in F Minor*; Mendelssohn: *Italian Symphony*
	7 November	Mozart: *Exultate Jubilate*; Elgar: *Enigma Variations*; Haydn: *Theresa Mass*
	12 December	Handel: *Messiah*

1968	12 March	Vivaldi: *Gloria*; Brahms: *St Antoni Variations*; Duruflé: *Requiem*
	12 November	Brahms: *Academic Festival Overture*; Dvorák: *Te Deum;* Mozart: *Symphony No 41* (Jupiter); Stravinsky: *Symphony of Psalms*
	10 December	Handel: *Messiah*

| 1969 | 11 March | Beethoven: *Missa Solemnis* |
| | 11 November | Mendelssohn: *Elijah* |

1970	14 March	Wagner: *Overture: Die Meistersinger von Nürnberg*; Elgar: *The Music Makers* (conducted by Sir Adrian Boult); Mozart: *Horn Concerto No 4* in E Flat; Britten: *Cantata Academica* (This was the so-called 'centenary' concert.)
	10 November	Tchaikovsky: *Romeo and Juliet* (fantasy overture); Honneger: *King David*
	8 December	Handel: *Messiah*

1971	9 March	Brahms: *Alto Rhapsody*; Brahms *Requiem*
	27 March	Rossini: *Petite Messe Solennelle*
	9 November	Elgar: *Introduction and Allegro for Strings*: Vaughan Williams: *A Sea Symphony*
	7 December	Handel: *Messiah*
1972	7 March	Handel: *Solomon*
	4 November	Haydn: *The Creation*
	5 December	Handel: *Messiah*
1973	17 March	Britten: *War Requiem*
	19 April	Bach: *St Matthew Passion*
	3 November	Monteverdi: *Vespers*
	4 December	Handel: *Messiah*
1974	9 March	Holst: *Hymn of Jesus*; Holst: *St Paul's Suite;* Verdi: *Four Sacred Pieces*
	2 November	Elgar: *The Dream of Gerontius*
	3 December	Handel: *Messiah*
1975	15 March	Bernstein: *Chichester Psalms*
		Mendelssohn: *Symphony No 2* (Hymn of Praise)
	1 November	Bruckner: *Te Deum*; Elgar: *Serenade for Strings*; Tippett: *A Child of our Time*
	2 December	Handel: *Messiah*
1976	13 March	Bach: *Mass in B Minor*
	6 November	Verdi: *Requiem*
	2 December	Handel: *Messiah*
1977	19 March	Poulenc: *Gloria*; Debussy: *Nocturnes*; Poulenc: *Stabat Mater*
	24 September	Herbert Howells: *Fanfare*; Elgar: *Prelude to the Kingdom* (conducted by Sir Adrian Boult); Elgar: *Cello Concerto* (soloist Paul Tortelier - conductor Sir Adrian Boult);Elgar: *The Music Makers* This was a special Elgar Foundation Celebrity Concert.
	12 November	Elgar: *Introduction and Allegro for Strings*; Vaughan Williams: *Sancta Civitas*; Walton: *Belshazzar's Feast*
	8 December	Handel: *Messiah*
1978	11 March	Bach: *St Matthew Passion*
	11 November	Britten: *War Requiem*
	7 December	Handel: *Messiah*
	16 December	Music for Christmas - a programme of carols
1979	10 March	Beethoven: *Missa Solemnis*
	17 November	Elgar: *The Kingdom*
	6 December	Handel: *Messiah*
	15 December	Carols for all
1980	22 March	Roxburgh: *The Rock*; Rossini: *Stabat Mater*
	19 June	Haydn: *Te Deum*; Mozart: *Symphony No 29* in A Major; Handel: *The King shall rejoice*; Handel: *The Water Music*; Handel: *Zadok the Priest*. Concert presented by WFCS in association with Cathedral Arts to commemorate the 1300th anniversary of the Diocese of Worcester.
	15 November	Brahms: *Variations on a Theme by Haydn*; *Requiem*
	4 December	Handel: *Messiah*
	13 December	Carols for all

1981	21 March	Elgar: *The Dream of Gerontius*
	2 June	Elgar: *Pomp and Circumstance March No 4;* Elgar: *Sea Pictures;* Elgar: *The Severn Suite;* Elgar: *The Music Makers* This was the Royal Elgar Concert on the occasion of the unveiling of the Elgar Statue by HRH The Prince of Wales.
	21 November	Holst: *Hymn of Jesus;* Williamson: *Mass of Christ the King*
1982	13 March	Cherubini: *Requiem;* Verdi: *Four Sacred Pieces*
	13 November	Mendelssohn: *Elijah*
	11 December	Bach: *Christmas Oratorio*
1983	19 March	Villette: *Messe en Français;* Poulenc: *Flute Concerto;* Fauré: *Requiem*
	19 November	Dvorák: *Requiem*
	9 December	Handel: *Messiah*
1984	23 February	Elgar: *The Dream of Gerontius*
	19 May	Dvorák: *Te Deum;* Elgar: *Enigma Variations;* Walton: *Belshazzar's Feast*
	24 November	Matthias: *Let us now praise famous men;* Vaughan Williams: *Fantasia on a theme of Thomas Tallis;* Elgar: *The Light of Life*
	6 December	Handel: *Messiah*
1985	23 March	Bach: *Mass in B Minor*
	23 November	Beethoven: *Missa Solemnis*
	5 December	Handel: *Messiah*
1986	15 March	Elgar: *Introduction and Allegro for Strings;* Copland: *Appalachian Spring;* Britten: *Spring Symphony*
	26 April	Vaughan Williams: *The Hundredth Psalm;* Mendelssohn: *Three Fantasias;* Mendelssohn: *Hear my prayer;* Fanshawe: *African Sanctus*
	22 November	Elgar: *The Apostles*
	2 December	Handel: *Messiah*
1987	21 March	Bach/Stravinsky: *Variations on Vom Himmel Hoch;* Stravinsky: *Concerto for piano and wind instruments;* Lloyd Webber: *Requiem*
	21 November	Mozart: *Symphony No 35* (Haffner); Mahler: *Das klagende Lied*
	8 December	Handel: *Messiah*
1988	19 March	Verdi: *Requiem*
	17 November	Elgar: *Overture Froissart;* Finzi: *Intimations of Immortality;* Elgar: *The Music Makers*
	10 December	Bach: *Christmas Oratorio*
1989	11 March	Haydn: *Te Deum;* Mozart: *Symphony No 40* in G Minor; Mozart: *Mass in C Minor*
	14 October	Walton: *Coronation March;* Von Suppé: *Overture - The Beautiful Galatea;* Elgar: *Elevation - Sursum Corda;* Fletcher: *Ring out wild bells;* Sibelius: *Tone Poem - Finlandia;* Richards: *County Scene;* Sparke: *Men of Harlech;* Handel: *Hallelujah Chorus;* King Henry VIII (arranged Roberts): *Pastime with good company;* Puccini: *Nessun Dorma;* Sullivan: *The Long Day Closes;* Adams: *The Holy City;* Wagner: *Procession to the Cathedral;* Steffe: *Battle Hymn of the Republic;* Elgar: *Pomp and Circumstance March No 1* For this performance, 'sounding brass and voices', WFCS were joined by the John Foster Black Dyke Mills Band.
	19 November	Bernstein: *Chichester Psalms;* Barber: *Adagio for Strings;* Hunt: *Te Deum;* Duruflé: *Requiem*
	9 December	Handel: *Messiah*

1990	24 March	Bach: *St Matthew Passion*
	17 November	Borodin: Overture and Polovtsian Dances from *Prince Igor*; Orff: *Carmina Burana*
1991	26 January	Handel: *Messiah*
	16 March	Sullivan: *Overture 'di Ballo'*; Coleridge-Taylor: *Hiawatha's Wedding Feast*; Elgar: *Cello Concerto*
	22 June	Allen: *March: Knight Templar*; Bernstein: *Overture: 'Candide'*; Strauss: *Tales from the Vienna Woods*; Lloyd: *English Heritage*; Brahe: *Bless this house*; Adams: *The Holy City*; Nilson: *Circius, Wind of the North*; Rogers/Hammerstein: Selections from *The King and I*; Sullivan: *The Lost Chord*; Lloyd: *Royal Parks*; Handel: *Hallelujah Chorus*; Parry: *Jerusalem* A 'Sounding Brass and Voices' Concert
	16 November	Mendelssohn: *Overture: The Hebrides*; Stanford: *Songs of the Fleet*; Vaughan Williams: *Sea Symphony*
	7 December	Handel: *Messiah*
1992	11 April	Honneger: *King David*
	17 October	Elgar: *The Kingdom*
	5 December	Handel: *Messiah*
	19 December	Celebration for Christmas
1993	10 March	Vaughan Williams: *Five mystical songs* and *Serenade to Music* (orchestral version) and Fauré: *Requiem*, all conducted by Sir David Willcocks; J Willcocks: *Voices of Time* (conducted by the composer).
	27 March	Williamson: *Procession of Palms*; Dupré: *Passion Symphony: Crucifixion*; Stainer: *The Crucifixion*
	6 November	Mendelssohn: *Elijah*
	4 December	Handel: *Messiah*
	18 December	'Joy to the World' - a concert of Christmas music
1994	26 March	Elgar: *The Dream of Gerontius*
	19 November	Bizet: *Te Deum*; Fauré: *Pavane;* Franck: *Psaume 150*; Berlioz: *Messe Solennelle*
	7 December	Handel: *Messiah*
	17 December	'Joy to the World' - a concert of Christmas music
1995	25 March	Bach: *Mass in B Minor*
	3 June	'A Celebration of Elgar's Music': including *Severn Suite*, Triumphal March from *Caractacus*, *Pomp & Circumstance March No.1*, *Wand of Youth Suite No. 1*, *From the Bavarian Highlands* (100th Annniversary performance).
	14 October	Atkins: *Hymn of Faith*; Julius Harrison: *Worcestershire Suite*; Hunt: *A Song of Celebration* (first performance); Elgar: *The Music Makers*
	9 December	Handel: *Messiah*
	16 December	'Joy to the World' - a concert of Christmas music

Bibliography

ATKINS, E Wulstan, *The Elgar-Atkins Friendship* (David and Charles,1985)

ATKINS, E Wulstan, *1890-1990, The Centenary of the Birth of a Friendship, Edward Elgar – Ivor Atkins* (published by the author, 1990)

BODEN, Anthony, *Three Choirs: A History of the Festival* (Alan Sutton Publishing Ltd, 1992)

MOORE, Jerrold Northrop, *Edward Elgar: A Creative Life* (Oxford, 1984)

MOORE, Jerrold Northrop, *Edward Elgar: Letters of a Lifetime* (Oxford, 1990)

SHAW, Harold Watkins, *The Three Choirs Festival* (Three Choirs/Ebenezer Baylis, 1954)

Index